MW01595832

Engaging Ethnographic Peace Research

While many have argued in the past decade that peace and conflict studies must engage more with local actors and communities, and scholars regularly describe the importance of local context and culture for building sustainable peace, there are substantial challenges methodologically to fulfilling this 'local turn'. Many peace and conflict studies scholars are inexperienced with methods appropriate for engaging with local communities, contexts, and cultures, and many of the important institutions in the field, from key journals to important funders, exhibit a continuing preference for quantitative studies.

The Ethnographic Peace Research (EPR) agenda has recently been developed in response to these challenges and is one of the key avenues to providing a methodological complement to the more theoretically focused local turn literature. This volume explores the application of the EPR approach in a number of post-conflict and conflict-affected societies around the world. While some chapters take a largely theoretical approach, most consider the practical application and the different kinds of methods that may be useful components of an EPR project. Together, the authors provide new insights into the benefits, challenges, and ethics of the emerging EPR agenda.

This book was originally published as a special issue of the journal *International Peacekeeping*.

Gearoid Millar is a Senior Lecturer of Sociology at the University of Aberdeen, UK. He studies the local experiences of international interventions for peace, justice, and development in post-conflict societies. He has developed the Ethnographic Peace Research (EPR) approach through his research projects on Transitional Justice, Peacebuilding, and Development in Sierra Leone.

Engaging Ethnographic Peace Research

Edited by
Gearoid Millar

 Routledge
Taylor & Francis Group

LONDON AND NEW YORK

First published 2019
by Routledge
2 Park Square, Milton Park, Abingdon, Oxon, OX14 4RN

and by Routledge
52 Vanderbilt Avenue, New York, NY 10017

Routledge is an imprint of the Taylor & Francis Group, an informa business

British Library Cataloguing-in-Publication Data
A catalogue record for this book is available from the British Library

ISBN13: 978-0-367-23678-6

Typeset in Minion Pro
by codeMantra

Publisher's Note
The publisher accepts responsibility for any inconsistencies that may have arisen during the conversion of this book from journal articles to book chapters, namely the possible inclusion of journal terminology.

Disclaimer
Every effort has been made to contact copyright holders for their permission to reprint material in this book. The publishers would be grateful to hear from any copyright holder who is not here acknowledged and will undertake to rectify any errors or omissions in future editions of this book.

Contents

Citation Information

The chapters in this book were originally published in the journal *International Peacekeeping*, volume 25, issue 5 (February 2018). When citing this material, please use the original page numbering for each article, as follows:

Chapter 1
Introduction: Engaging Ethnographic Peace Research: Exploring an Approach
Gearoid Millar
International Peacekeeping, volume 25, issue 5 (February 2018) pp. 597–609

Chapter 2
Visiting the Tiger Zone – Methodological, Conceptual and Ethical Challenges of Ethnographic Research on Perpetrators
Timothy Williams
International Peacekeeping, volume 25, issue 5 (February 2018) pp. 610–629

Chapter 3
With Soymilk to the Khmer Rouge: Challenges of Researching Ex-combatants in Post-war Contexts
Anne Hennings
International Peacekeeping, volume 25, issue 5 (February 2018) pp. 630–652

Chapter 4
Ethnographic Peace Research: The Underappreciated Benefits of Long-term Fieldwork
Gearoid Millar
International Peacekeeping, volume 25, issue 5 (February 2018) pp. 653–676

Chapter 5
Suspicion and Ethnographic Peace Research (Notes from a Local Researcher)
Nerve Valerio Macaspac
International Peacekeeping, volume 25, issue 5 (February 2018) pp. 677–694

Chapter 6

Critiquing Anthropological Imagination in Peace and Conflict Studies: From Empiricist Positivism to a Dialogical Approach in Ethnographic Peace Research
Philipp Lottholz
International Peacekeeping, volume 25, issue 5 (February 2018) pp. 695–720

For any permission-related enquiries please visit:
http://www.tandfonline.com/page/help/permissions

Notes on Contributors

Anne Hennings is a Research Fellow at the University of Münster, Germany. She researches social movements and contentious politics in post-war societies with special emphasis on land conflicts. Based on extensive ethnographic fieldwork in Cambodia and Sierra Leone, she explores the risks of contested land deals for conflict transformation. She is co-founder and speaker of the working group 'Nature, Resources, Conflict' and editor of the www.resources-and-conflict.org blog.

Philipp Lottholz is a Post-Doctoral Research Fellow at the DFG Collaborative Research Centre/Transregio 138 "Dynamics of Security" and the Institute of Sociology at Justus Liebig University of Giessen, Germany. His research interests include political sociology, critical peacebuilding studies, practice-based and action/activist methodology, international political economy, post-Socialist/post-Soviet studies, and postcolonial and decolonial international studies.

Nerve Valerio Macaspac is an Assistant Professor of Geography in the Department of Political Science and Global Affairs at the College of Staten Island at the City University of New York (CUNY), USA, where he teaches Geographic Information Systems (GIS) and Urban Geography. His research examines the maintenance of community-led demilitarized geographic areas, popularly known as peace zones, during armed conflict to better understand peace beyond the dominant definition as absence of violence, and peacebuilding as a state-centric or expert-driven project of conflict resolution.

Gearoid Millar is a Senior Lecturer of Sociology at the University of Aberdeen, UK. He studies the local experiences of international interventions for peace, justice, and development in post-conflict societies. He has developed the Ethnographic Peace Research (EPR) approach through his research projects on Transitional Justice, Peacebuilding, and Development in Sierra Leone. He has published articles in the *Journal of Peace Research*, *International Peacekeeping*, the *Journal of Human Rights*, *Cooperation and Conflict*, the *Journal of Agrarian Change*, *Rural Sociology*, and *Third World Quarterly*.

Timothy Williams is a Postdoctoral Research Fellow at the Centre for Conflict Studies at Marburg University, Germany. Here he also concluded his PhD in 2017 (*summa cum laude*) and has since been acknowledged with two awards, one by the university of Marburg, the other by the German Peace Psychologist Association. His research deals with violence, focussing on its dynamics, particularly at the micro-level, as well as its consequences for post-conflict societies. He has conducted extensive field research in Cambodia, as well as Armenia and Rwanda and has been awarded the Emerging Scholar Prize of the International Association of Genocide Scholars in 2017.

Engaging Ethnographic Peace Research: Exploring an Approach

Gearoid Millar

ABSTRACT
As has been thoroughly rehearsed in the literature, the failures of the liberal peace model of post-conflict intervention have given rise to a 'local turn' in peace research. This in turn has refocused attention away from the motivations and practices of international actors towards local ownership and 'buy-in', and the importance of culture, context, and 'the Everyday'. There is a mismatch, however, between the methodological skills among peace researchers today, and the new imperative to explore local and everyday understandings, perceptions, and experiences of conflict, transition, and peace. For this reason a number of scholars have recently emphasized the importance of incorporating ethnographic methods and an anthropological imagination into peace research. However, at this point, and as evidenced in the contributions to this special issue, there are many challenges to such incorporation which must be acknowledge and addressed if the ethnographic approach is to fulfil its early promise to add empirical substance to the local turn. The contributing authors each address different challenges to conducting Ethnographic Peace Research (EPR) in post-conflict contexts and, as this introduction argues, they evidence clearly the variety of questions yet to be answered while suggesting different ways ethnographic approaches can be incorporated into peace research.

Introduction

There are few today who doubt the failures of the 'peace industry' to success-fully establish sustainable peace in a variety of post-conflict contexts.[1] The 'liberal peace' model has been roundly criticised as overly technocratic and disconnected from the needs of local people in post-conflict settings.[2] There is little doubt today that post-conflict interventions for the purpose of building peace require some engagement with 'the local'. Most scholars recognize therefore that, at a bare minimum, knowledge of the sub-national context is

---

[1]Mac Ginty, "Routine Peace," 289.
[2]Mac Ginty, "Hybrid Peace"; Millar, "Local Experiences of Justice"; Autesserre, *Peaceland*.

necessary for the design, planning, and eventual implementation of peace interventions. However, going beyond this minimum, others would argue that successful peacebuilding will require engaging with, consulting, incorporating, or even empowering local actors and institutions within that context,[3] while still others may call for international actors to actually withdraw to a great degree from such processes, serving more as supporters and facilitators of a locally driven peace.[4] This turn to the local has inspired substantial reflection in the field and how we should define, research, and engage with the local are still open questions.[5] One suggestion, however, has been that a turn to ethnographic methods can provide some leverage on these questions.[6]

As I describe in my contribution to this Special Issue, such an approach has substantial precedent in the field of Anthropology. Many anthropologists have examined the dynamics of conflict and violence,[7] as well as local and community experiences of post-conflict transition and peace.[8] Such work has illustrated the value of ethnographic methods in understanding the everyday experiences of conflict and post-conflict dynamics and, perhaps more importantly, the diversity and intricacy of those experiences across contexts and cultures. However, as Bräuchler notes, what she terms the 'cultural turn' in peace and conflict studies has so far been dominated by scholars of political science, international relations, and legal studies who are largely unaware of the theoretical depth and conceptual nuance of either 'culture' or 'the local' as they have developed within the field of Anthropology.[9] She argues, in short, that scholars working within these disciplines are unprepared theoretically to engage in ethnographic research. I have further noted in earlier work that these same disciplines (to which I would add also the discipline of economics), are also those in which 'extended fieldwork has not traditionally been considered necessary in order to understand a problem even if that problem is located in societies and cultures wholly unlike those of the researcher'.[10] Together, therefore, these contributions highlighted the conceptual and methodological unpreparedness to engage with 'the local' via ethnographic methods among the great majority of peace researchers today.

It was partly in response to this challenge that I initiated the Ethnographic Peace Research (EPR) project in late 2015, and encouraged active peace scholars to submit papers which would illustrate, promote, or question the use of ethnographic methods in Peace Research. The goal was to solicit

---

[3]Mac Ginty and Richmond, "Local Turn," 770.
[4]Ali and Matthews, "Durable Peace," 408.
[5]Paffenholz, "Unpacking the Local"; Hughes, Öjendal, and Schierenbeck, "Struggle"; and Randazzo, "Paradoxes of the Everyday."
[6]Mac Ginty and Richmond, "Fallacy," 5.
[7]Richards, *Fighting*; Nordstrom, *Shadows*; de Waal, *Real Politics*.
[8]Das, *Life and Words*; Honwana, *Child Soldiers*; Theidon, *Intimate Enemies*.
[9]Bräuchler, *Cultural Dimension*.
[10]Millar, *Ethnographic Approach*, 135.

contributions from scholars from across the disciplinary spectrum who self-identified as already engaged in EPR and who could, therefore, address questions regarding the strengths, challenges, and ethics of the 'ethnographic turn'. The articles included in this Special Issue, as well as chapters already published in a recent edited volume,[11] were submitted in response to this initial call and certainly do take some tentative initial steps towards answering these question. However, addressing the strengths, challenges, and ethics of an EPR approach has turned out to be more difficult than initially considered. Indeed, the sub-title of the edited volume slowly morphed from 'Strengths, Challenges, and Ethics' to 'Approaches and Tensions' as it became clear that thinking about, designing and deploying ethnographic methods for peace research proved to be a contentious undertaking, sparking tensions between Anthropologists and non-Anthropologists involved in the project.[12] The contributions to this Special Issue evidence some similar tensions, while also unearthing others. However, I argue here that it is exactly the work of uncovering and exploring these tensions which will help develop and consolidate a robust EPR agenda.

Engaging Ethnographic Peace Research

I use the term 'engaging' in the title of this introduction specifically because it can have two meanings. It can refer to the manner in which the contributing scholars engaged in the practice of ethnographic research (how they each collected their data), as well as to the manner in which they engage with the ideas which underpin the approach (how they then think about how they collected their data). The five articles evince some diversity of practice, which contributes, in turn, to varied reflections on the strengths and limitations of the approach. My own contribution to this special issue was initiated by the need I felt to more fully examine the difference between the way I have been thinking about EPR (which to me has always demanded long-term engagement with the local context and people) and the kind of processes I often see labelled as 'ethnographic' (which often consists of interviews conducted during a few short weeks of 'fieldwork'). The problem with the latter, I argue in my article, is that the researcher does not gain a deep enough knowledge of the local sociocultural context during such short trips, which, in turn, hinders their ability to ask appropriate questions or interpret the answers they receive. I argue that it is 'only with sufficient time in the setting that the researcher can come to understand the situated concepts which underpin experiences of conflict, transition, and peace in post-conflict societies' and an understanding of exactly these concepts is

---

[11]Millar, *Ethnographic Peace Research*.
[12]Ibid., 261–5.

necessary to 'assess both local expectations for and the local experiences of peace intervention'. The article first provides a brief discussion of the local turn in peace research, and then a short review of Anthropological contributions regarding the dynamics of conflict, post-conflict recovery and peace. It then then turns to a discussion of the three key benefits of long-term fieldwork, which set EPR as I define it (as requiring such long-term engagement) apart from purely short-term 'field-trip' based interview research. Based on reflections from more than 19 months of fieldwork over two projects,[13] I describe these varied benefits under the headings of time, chance and change.

Each of these benefits is illustrated with a few examples. The benefits of time are illustrated with examples of the greater amount of knowledge regarding and engagement with the people and communities I was studying, as well as the methodological value gained via second translations of my interviews which revealed new and important data but would have been impossible without sufficient time, and of the evolution of my research methodology generally over the course of my fieldwork. The benefits of serendipity, or chance, are also clearly related to additional time in the field, I argue, and can be seen in the increasing likelihood that anyone spending substantial time in a setting will be more likely to interact with a more varied array of actors and institutions, and to experience all of the good and the bad that might befall one in that society; from medical emergencies to security problems. As I argue in the article, those in country for only a few weeks and staying in high-end hotels, travelling in air-conditioned vehicles, and interviewing fellow elites will have little chance to experience the serendipitous events that provide so much insight into the daily struggles of average people in transitional societies. Finally, the benefits of change are illustrated both by the added insight into local socioeconomic and political dynamics evidenced by the changes between my first period of fieldwork in 2008/2009 and my return for a second project in 2012. Over this time the economic and social situation in and around the northern Sierra Leonean town of Makeni where I conduct my research – and the engagement by external actors in this setting – changed substantially and altered the local understandings, perceptions, and experiences of international interventions. I argue in my contribution, therefore, that there are insights to be gained by long-term EPR which are not accessible by those utilizing more short-term interview based methodologies.

As reported in their respective contributions, both Williams and Hennings conducted such long-term projects in the post-conflict context of Cambodia, and both even sampled from and interviewed former members of the Khmer

---

[13]Millar, "Between Western Theory"; Millar, "Expectations and Experiences"; Millar, "Investing in Peace"; and Millar, "Local Experiences of Liberal."

Rouge during their fieldwork. However, the actual methodological processes they followed were quite distinct. The focus of their studies led them to sample their interlocutors in different ways, from different regions, and for the purpose of asking quite different questions. Williams was specifically focusing on the motivations which lead actors to participate in genocide, and sought to collect data among former Khmer Rouge cadres to test a framework for understanding such motivations which he calls the 'complexity of evil' model. Hennings' study, on the other hand, was more focused on the present and the 'micro-politics of contestation against land grabbing in post-conflict settings and its potential repercussions on conflict transformation'. As such, while both studies examine sensitive topics, they required different methodologies of data collection and generated different forms of tension.

Williams' research question required him to focus particularly on non-elite former perpetrators and their understandings of and their motivations for supporting Democratic Kampuchea (the name given to Cambodia by the Khmer Rouge at the time). As his article outlines, his research process, while distinct from traditional notions of Anthropological fieldwork, nonetheless sought to uncover the deeply contextualized motivations of non-elite actors for participation in collective violence. As such, he faced a number of substantial challenges, including: (1) the difficulty of identifying former cadres to speak to, as in some areas of the country there are few social networks of such former combatants; (2) the problem of overcoming the tendency for former combatants to 'avoid honest responses' in order to 'dissociate themselves' from their previous actions; (3) the potential stigmatization of participants who might be identified by their new communities due to their participation in the research; (4) ethical concerns about what to do with any potentially incriminating evidence that might be uncovered during the research; and (5) the problem of framing former combatants inherently as perpetrators within the context of the project while they predominantly saw themselves as victims.

Given these specific challenges, the principle argument forwarded by Williams' in his article is that more traditionally Anthropological fieldwork based on long-term residence and embeddedness within a single community would have been less useful than the less embedded process of repeat visits to various communities and interviews with specific individuals which he chose to deploy. While Williams recognizes that the traditional embeddedness of long-term fieldwork can provide for rich insights into the local context, he also argues that it would contribute to the risk of exposing his interviewees to stigmatization within the community. As his interviewees were not all located in 'stronghold' communities where most people were supporters of the Khmer Rouge, but in more diverse communities, long-term embeddedness would mean that many more people would know the purpose of his research and therefore that his interlocutors were former low-level Khmer Rouge cadres. Williams argues, therefore, that while a less embedded process certainly has some weaknesses – it does not, for example, allow a researcher 'to trace specific networks in one location or build up one local history' – it did allow him to explore his research question with a diverse array of former perpetrators over his six months of fieldwork while avoiding the challenges of exposure and self-incrimination that might have faced interlocutors during a more embedded process.

Although set in the same country and engaging with members of the same former armed group, Hennings study is quite different in that it focuses not on motivations for past membership and violence, but on the potential repercussions for the post-conflict stability of a very contemporary problem. Specifically, her study sought to explore the opinions about and reactions to land-grabbing among former Khmer Rouge cadres (both low and high level) and thus to use this 'emphasis on ex-combatants' … 'as a lens to uncover potential risks of land grabbing for peace and stability in post-conflict environments'. As a result, this research focus led to a more methodologically diverse approach to ethnography. Hennings describes her 'methods repertoire' as including non-structured interviews, dialogues, informal discussions, and participatory observation with staff of specific non-governmental organizations and the UN as well as monks, officials, activists, and communities affected by land grabbing. While Williams largely conducted life-history interviews with his interlocutors to explore their motivations for past actions, Hennings was using this more diverse array of methods to focus on the 'motivations and strategies of everyday resistance, overt advocacy politics, and official resistance', which reminds us that all such methodological choices must reflect the phenomena under study. Like Williams, however, Hennings also notes the challenges inherent in such research and her article echoes his concern with the micro-social context of identifying and approaching interlocutors. However, to Hennings, who focused more of her time and effort over 12 months of fieldwork in the 'stronghold' communities, spending substantial time in the communities to develop trust and rapport was 'pivotal both to identify and access ex-combatants'; the direct inverse of Williams' response.

While a substantial contribution of her article focuses on the importance of focusing on these micro-dynamics of building trust in post-conflict research, including reflections on her own positionality as a young, white, female scholar, Hennings also discusses the more practical challenges of researching a sensitive political topic in a post-conflict environment. She describes the travel times associated with avoiding exclusion zones due to mines or military checkpoints, having to change plans at the last minute due to the security concerns of her interlocutors, and the problematic dynamics of doing research 'under-the-radar' which led her to sometimes feel rushed and threatened.

In addition, she provides an extremely interesting discussion of the role of and the trials faced by her research assistants during this process, who, she argues, proved pivotal in overcoming barriers to access and trust, but may also face daunting personal challenges related to the research question or their personal experiences of the past violence. In short, this article outlines the challenges to EPR within still-sensitive, increasingly restrictive post-conflict countries, and particularly among former combatants when their engagement with politics is still a key fear of the new government. Her findings point to the importance of both 'intuition and ethics' as well as careful reflection on the part of the researcher regarding their status, role, privilege and identity, in all of the steps of the research process.

Coming from a completely different angle, case, and question, Macaspac's contribution nonetheless takes up Hennings' call for careful reflection in its focus on the experience of local ethnographers studying conflict dynamics in their country of origin. Specifically, in this article Macaspac examines the role 'suspicion' can play as a lens to understand the distinct challenges such researchers face, arguing that the ways in which locals conducting research become objects of (and face consequences from) suspicion during fieldwork sets their research process and experience apart from that of researchers from outside the context. These reflections emerge from his experiences as a Filipino researcher conducting an ethnographic study of how communities make peace 'beyond the purview of the state' in the Philippines and within the context of an ongoing Maoist rebellion. As he argues, local researchers examining such sensitive issues face quite daunting challenges international researchers rarely face. Because they are locals, for example, such researchers are subject to national and local laws from which international researchers may enjoy protections. They cannot rely on their passports, on embassies and consulates, or simply on their white skin to rescue them from state surveillance, harassment and intimidation. Further, their deeper roots in the community means that their families and friends can also be targeted by such measures and of course their 'current or future professional careers can be jeopardized'. As Macaspac describes, in various contexts (including the Philippines) researchers have been killed and disappeared and regularly face harassment 'through overt forms of surveillance that are meant to intimidate'.

But local researchers are actually further disadvantaged in this dynamic as they face what Macaspac describes as 'double suspicion'. Not only do they face the consequences of suspicion in their research site – which impacts on how they engage and build trust with local individuals and institutions who are often 'ambivalent towards the role of Western education' – but they also face suspicion from the wider academic community. Western scholars, he argues, 'suspect the intellectual contributions of local researchers' who are expected to 'demonstrate scholarly distance and defamiliarize their knowledge of their own countries and communities'. In many scholarly traditions, he argues, ignorance or 'cultural blindness' is seen as necessary for true discovery and important insights. Being too familiar, in such a tradition, means that local researchers will 'be less attentive to the banal and taken-for-granted features of the culture itself', which is thought to be central to uncovering new knowledge. The attempt by local ethnographers, however, to embody the values of the objective, neutral or disengaged researcher when studying violence and conflict in their countries of origin, is ironically, 'what renders local researchers objects of suspicion among the civilian communities they study'. This contribution, therefore, describes both the strengths and challenges of conducting EPR as a local ethnographer, while also highlighting the privileges enjoyed by international researchers and how discourses regarding 'good' research 'often conceal white normativity and Western-centric discourses behind a set of universal claims over objective scholarship'.

Although focusing on different problems, Macaspac's critique complements that from Lottholz, whose article presents a forceful indictment of 'the reception and conceptualization of ethnography' in the field of peace research. To Lottholz ethnographic work within peace research has been dominated by an 'empiricist positivism and a preference of [sic] theory building and testing over in-depth research'. While I would contest this generalization of the use of ethnography in the field more broadly, Lottholz's identification of a positivist tendency within EPR as I have presented it in the past,[14] when combined with the 'peace prerogative' – or the normative aspect of peace studies as a discipline seeking to contribute to the building of peaceful societies – may indeed render it, as he describes, 'complicit in the instantiation of negative and imperial forms of peace'. This argument, which takes up a substantial part of Lottholz's contribution, is generally that the presentation of ethnographic methods as a tool by which the researcher can approximate 'the "real" empirical situation' on the ground in order to 'enable the best possible understanding of the effects (and shortcomings) of peacebuilding interventions' ... 'forecloses discussion about how peacebuilding is embedded in, extends and re-produces a global web of power relations' and potentially provides evidence to support and facilitate new forms of power. To Lottholz this evidences the disinterest among local turn and ethnographic scholars in the actual dynamics of local societies and shows the claim to provide voice and agency to local actors to be little more than a scholarly conceit.

He argues, in response, that those writing on the 'local turn' and claiming to use ethnographic approaches must take more seriously the central lessons of the Writing Culture and Third World Feminism debates in order to truly incorporate a contemporary Anthropological perspective. To Lottholz this

---

[14]Millar, *Ethnographic Approach.*

necessitates a 're-negotiation and transgression of the traditional boundaries between scholarship, practice and activism' and, as he proposes and describes with reflections from his own fieldwork in Kyrgyzstan, it demands that peace scholars develop research which fully incorporates local actors as equal partners in a process of 'collaborative knowledge production'. He further claims that such research must focus not on everyday forms of peace, as many local turn scholars would encourage,[15] but on everyday forms of conflict which, he argues 'are often more present in and impeding on people's lives'. In Lottholz' perception, EPR cannot make a real contribution to the study of peace and conflict if it excludes 'voices and events' which depart from an idealized picture of a peaceful society. He argues, therefore, in his article, that this is what much peace scholarship does, excluding, silencing, downplaying, or actually denying alternative narratives 'out of a longing for peace'. Lottholz therefore argues that his own approach to collaborative research overcomes the extractive nature of such positivist ethnographic work by working with partners, thus having the potential to 'forge a dialogue with practitioners'.

Conclusion: Defining Ethnographic Peace Research

The contributions in this Special Issue, therefore, evidence the tensions that arise when different scholars deploy diverse methods in distinct contexts to answer varying questions regarding conflict, transition, and peace. From the positive portrayals of Williams and Hennings, to the more problematizing work of my own paper and that of Macaspac, and then the heavily critical piece from Lottholz, we see a range of different ideas regarding the strengths, challenges and ethics of EPR. But perhaps more importantly, we see very different approaches to even assessing these characteristics. This diversity of perspectives echoes a similar diversity and tension which emerged in the related edited volume, which, over 10 chapters, presented more than a dozen EPR studies.[16] In that case the most substantial tension was apparent between a number of the non-Anthropologist contributors who were proposing that EPR can best be deployed as an actively collaborative or activist process,[17] and the participating Anthropologists who saw ethnographic work as an inherently collaborative production of knowledge between the researcher and their interlocutors but generally resisted this activist role for EPR.[18]

Interestingly this seems to directly call into question Lottholz's contention that a more up-to-date or contemporary approach to EPR must be an 'activist' form of research as it was the Anthropologists most in tune with ethnography

---

[15]Williams, "Reproducing Everyday Peace"; Mac Ginty, "Everyday Peace."

[16]Millar, *Ethnographic Peace Research.*

[17]Klein, "Institutional Ethnography"; Collins and Watson, "Impetus for Peace Studies"; Close, "Researching Peace Peacefully."

[18]Bräuchler, "Contextualizing"; Sakti and Reynaud, "Understanding Reconciliation."

in its post-Writing Culture, post-Third World Feminism form who resisted such conceptions of EPR. There are tensions, therefore, between the idea of EPR as an empirical, evaluative or analytic process (which is certainly how I would define my own approach to date), and EPR as an activist project. But while Lottholz seems to want to see the former as open to instrumentalization by powerful forces and the latter not, I would argue that neither should be considered free of this danger. Indeed, the inequality of power and diversity of motivations among national, sub-national and local actors and institutions should make it apparent that even collaborative work alongside local actors and within local institutions can be turned to the purpose of power and the marginalization of sub-groups. It is for this reason that conducting rigorous and nuanced ethnographic research must involve a constant awareness of the operation of power and attention not to *either* everyday peace or everyday conflict, but to the manner in which these interact among and between different actors and institutions.

In the already completed edited volume I concluded with a definition of EPR which proposed that it be defined by two required characteristics which I described as *thick description* and an attempt to *understand how and why* in addition to simply what one is observing. I then proposed that there are also two facilitative characteristics which are not strictly necessary but greatly enhance the rigour and nuance of EPR, which were *reflexivity* and a *diversity of potential data collection methods*.[19] It is clear, at this point, that all five of the articles included here provide further evidence for the importance of these four characteristics, and, indeed, the articles by Macaspac and Hennings would both seem to indicate that reflexivity and a diversity of potential data collection methods (what Hennings discussed as her 'methods repertoire') may be quite important indeed. The final characteristic, however, was described not as required, nor as facilitative, but as a potential; as something that should be considered as one way that peace scholars might engage in EPR, but certainly not as the only way that they may do so. This is the inclusion of *collaborative or emancipatory* goals and processes. This echoes the way that such research has been incorporated into Anthropology. While many have promoted Action Research or Applied Anthropology, it has certainly not been taken as the only or even the primary way to conduct research in that field.[20] Many in Anthropology have felt quite ambivalent towards such an approach,[21] and this is true also in peace studies, as evidenced by the tension described above.

The path forward for EPR, therefore, is not quite clear, but perhaps we can say that while the first four characteristics are clearly important for the design

---

[19]Millar, *Ethnographic Peace Research*, 258–60.
[20]Tax, "Action Anthropology"; Schensul et al., "Core Elements."
[21]Rubinstein, "Reflections on Action Anthropology."

and application of rigorous EPR projects, this fifth requires substantive consideration and perhaps application only to specific cases and contexts. There are as many negative potentials with action research as there are positive, and quite a lot depends on the motivations and intentions of actors and institutions, which scholars are often only coming to know when they enter the field. At the very least, the vagaries of such a form of EPR would require substantially more investigation and planning before fieldwork begins, as well as constant reflection and critical appraisal of the dynamics of power while in the field. Deciding what cases and contexts are appropriate for such studies, and what actors and institutions are or are not appropriate partners for such projects, must be the task of individual scholars engaging in their own EPR adventures. Certainly we are not at a point where it is responsible to say that all EPR must be activist EPR. Quite to the contrary, we have barely begun to discuss and examine the potential strengths, challenges and ethics of EPR and much remains to be done.

Disclosure Statement

No potential conflict of interest was reported by the author.

Bibliography

Ali, Taisier M., and Robert O. *Matthews. Durable Peace: Challenges for Peacebuilding in Africa*. Toronto: University of Toronto Press, 2004.

Autesserre, Severine. *Peaceland: Conflict Resolution and the Everyday Politics of International Intervention*. New York: Cambridge University Press, 2014.

Bräuchler, Birgit. *The Cultural Dimension of Peace: Decentralization and Reconciliation in Indonesia*. Basingstoke: Palgrave MacMillan, 2015.

Bräuchler, Birgit. "Contextualizing Ethnographic Peace Research." in *Ethnographic Peace Research: Approaches and Tensions*, ed. Gearoid Millar, 21–42. Basingstoke: Palgrave MacMillan, 2018.

Close, Sophia. "Researching Peace Peacefully: Using Ethnographic Approaches in Timor-Leste." in *Ethnographic Peace Research: Approaches and Tensions*, ed. Gearoid Millar, 181–206. Basingstoke: Palgrave MacMillan, 2018.

Collins, Bennett, and Alison Watson. "The Impetus for Peace Studies to Make a Collaborative Turn: Towards Community Collaborative Research." in *Ethnographic Peace Research: Approaches and Tensions*, ed. Gearoid Millar, 89–114. Basingstoke: Palgrave MacMillan, 2018.

Das, Veena. *Life and Words: Violence and the Descent into the Ordinary*. Berkeley: University of California Press, 2007.

De Waal, Alex. *The Real Politics of the Horn of Africa: Money, War and the Business of Power*. Cambridge: Polity Press, 2015.

Honwana, Alcinda. *Child Soldiers in Africa*. Philadelphia: University of Pennsylvania Press, 2006.

Hughes, Caroline, Joakim Öjendal and Isabell Schierenbeck. "The Struggle and the Song – The Local Turn in Peacebuilding: An Introduction." *Third World Quarterly* 36, no. 5 (2015): 817–24.

Klein, Mike. "Institutional Ethnography as Peace Research." in *Ethnographic Peace Research: Approaches and Tensions*, ed. Gearoid Millar, 65–88. Basingstoke: Palgrave MacMillan, 2018.

Mac Ginty, Roger. "Hybrid Peace: The Interaction between Top-Down and Bottom-Up Peace." *Security Dialogue* 41, no. 4 (2010): 391–412.

Mac Ginty, Roger. "Routine Peace: Technocracy and Peacebuilding." *Cooperation and Conflict* 47, no. 3 (2012): 287–308.

Mac Ginty, Roger. "Everyday Peace: Bottom-Up and Local Agency in Conflict-Affected Societies." *Security Dialogue* 45, no. 6 (2014): 548–64.

Mac Ginty, Roger and Oliver P. Richmond. "The Local Turn in Peace Building: A Critical Agenda for Peace." *Third World Quarterly* 34, no. 5 (2013): 763–83.

Mac Ginty, Roger and Oliver P. Richmond. "The Fallacy of Constructing Hybrid Political Orders: A Reappraisal of the Hybrid Turn in Peacebuilding." *International Peacekeeping* 23, no. 2 (2016): 219–39.

Millar, Gearoid. "Local Evaluations of Justice through Truth Telling in Sierra Leone: Postwar Needs and Transitional Justice." *Human Rights Review* 12, no. 4 (2011): 515–35.

Millar, Gearoid. "Between Western Theory and Local Practice: Cultural Impediments to Truth-Telling in Sierra Leone." *Conflict Resolution Quarterly* 29, no. 2 (2012): 177–99.

Millar, Gearoid. "Expectations and Experiences of Peacebuilding in Sierra Leone: Parallel Peacebuilding Processes and Compound Friction." *International Peacekeeping* 20, no. 2 (2013): 189–203.

Millar, Gearoid. *An Ethnographic Approach to Peacebuilding: Understanding Local Experiences in Transitional States*. London: Routledge, 2014.

Millar, Gearoid. "Investing in Peace: Foreign Direct Investment as Economic Restoration in Sierra Leone?" *Third World Quarterly* 36, no. 9 (2015): 1700–16.

Millar, Gearoid. "Local Experiences of Liberal Peace: Marketization and Emergent Conflict Dynamics in Sierra Leone." *Journal of Peace Research* 53, no. 4 (2016): 569–81.

Millar, Gearoid. *Ethnographic Peace Research: Approaches and Tensions*. Basingstoke: Palgrave MacMillan, 2018.

Nordstrom, Carolyn. *Shadows of War: Violence, Power, and International Profiteering in the Twenty-First Century*. Berkeley: University of California Press, 2004.

Paffenholz, Thania. "Unpacking the Local Turn in Peacebuilding: A Critical Assessment towards an Agenda for Future Research." *Third World Quarterly* 36, no. 5 (2015): 857–74.

Randazzo, Elisa. "The Paradoxes of the 'Everyday': Scrutinising the Local Turn in Peace Building." *Third World Quarterly* 37, no. 8 (2016): 1351–70.

Richards, Paul. *Fighting for the Rainforest: War, Youth & Resources in Sierra Leone*. Portsmouth: Heinemann, 1996.

Rubenstein, Robert A. "Reflections on Action Anthropology: Some Developmental Dynamics of an Anthropological Tradition." *Human Organization* 45, no. 3 (1986): 270–9.

Sakti, Victoria K., and Anne-Marie Reynaud. "Understanding Reconciliation through Reflexive Practice: Ethnographic Examples from Canada and Timor-Leste." in *Ethnographic Peace Research: Approaches and Tensions*, ed. Gearoid Millar, 159–180. Basingstoke: Palgrave MacMillan, 2018.

Schensul, Jean, Marlene Berg, Daniel Schensul, and Sandra Syndlo. "Core Elements of Participatory Action Research for Educational Empowerment and Risk Prevention in Urban Youth." *Practicing Anthropology* 26, no. 2 (2004): 5–9.

Tax, Sol. "Action Anthropology." *Current Anthropology* 16, no. 4 (1975): 514–17.
Thiedon, Kimberly. *Intimate Enemies: Violence and Reconciliation in Peru.* Philadelphia: University of Pennsylvania Press, 2013.
Williams, Philippa. "Reproducing Everyday Peace in North India: Process, Politics, and Power." *Annals of the Association of American Geographers* 103, no. 1 (2013): 230–50.

Visiting the Tiger Zone – Methodological, Conceptual and Ethical Challenges of Ethnographic Research on Perpetrators

Timothy Williams

ABSTRACT

This article is a methodological, conceptual and ethical reflection on challenges and opportunities afforded to ethnographic researchers in the field when working with perpetrators of mass violence and their motivations. Departing from a research project on the motivations of former cadres of the Khmer Rouge and fieldwork conducted on this topic in Cambodia, various possible approaches to conducting such ethnographic research are discussed, focusing on long-term stays in the community, frequent visits and building networks in the community, and repeat individual visits to select people without embedding oneself as a researcher in the community. For each of these approaches their distinct strengths and limitations are considered in light of various methodological, conceptual and ethical challenges encountered by the author in the field. As such, this article does not suggest specific methodological developments but offers a critical reflection of how various approaches to an ethnography of perpetrators can variously deal with these challenges.

Introduction

When we joined [the Khmer Rouge] it was like we were entering into a tiger zone, so we had to be a tiger like them. If not, they could take us to be killed. Even if we were the same soldiers of Pol Pot, if we made a mistake, they would also take us to be killed. So we needed to be a tiger like them, to be cruel like them. No morality like them. That's why they were like that.[1]

This former cadre of the Khmer Rouge described the environment he was entering when he joined the organization as the tiger zone and knew that when he entered this tiger zone that he himself would have to become a tiger. By becoming a tiger, he recognized that he would have to think like a tiger and behave like a tiger. That is, he would have to take on the values, attitudes and behavioural patterns of a tiger. Using this metaphor of the tiger

---

[1] Interview with a former militiaman [*chhlop*], later also militia group leader in August 2014 in Battambang province, Cambodia.

zone, this person explained what it was like for him when he joined the totalitarian and violent organization of the Khmer Rouge and how he immediately understood what it meant to be a Khmer Rouge cadre.

This passage is taken from an interview which was part of a research project in which I sought to understand the motivations of ordinary Cambodian men and women to join the Khmer Rouge and in their roles participate in the use of violence (as opposed to elite-centric research on the leaders of the Khmer Rouge, such as Pol Pot or Duch).[2] This research is part of a comparative project in which insights from Cambodia, Rwanda, the Holocaust and other cases have been synthesized to the *Complexity of Evil* model. In the process of conducting this research project, I was confronted with numerous challenges in approaching former cadres of the Khmer Rouge and talking to them about their everyday lives under the regime, their paths into the organization and further into violence and their motivations for this.

These challenges may come as no surprise given the extremely sensitive nature of the topic, but for an in-depth understanding of perpetrators and their motivations they need to be overcome. This piece provides a reflection on these challenges of conducting fieldwork with former perpetrators of mass violence along some methodological, conceptual and ethical lines. I have titled the article 'Visiting the Tiger Zone' because it draws on six months of fieldwork which I conducted in 10 provinces of Cambodia from July 2014 to January 2015. This 'tiger zone' refers not to a specific region in Cambodia with a high density of former Khmer Rouge, although I did interview people in the former stronghold areas of the city of Pailin in Pailin Province, as well as the districts of Kamrieng and Phnom Proek in Battambang province, all along the border to Thailand. 'Visiting the tiger zone' refers more to the fact that I came as a researcher to speak with these former Khmer Rouge cadres and to delve into their understandings of Democratic Kampuchea, as the state was called under the Khmer Rouge regime; the visiting also refers to the fact that I was not there with them on a permanent basis.

While the problems described in this article are discussed for the Cambodian case, many of the dynamics exist for other cases also. Most previous work on the Cambodian genocide has not focused specifically on the motivations of individual perpetrators,[3] but has been on broader historical dynamics, making it relatively *terra nova* for the case and necessitating drawing on other cases for inspiration on how to overcome the challenges. As such, the article draws strongly on the methodological repertoire of scholars who have pursued similar questions in Rwanda and the Holocaust, where most of the previous research on why people participate in genocide has been conducted. Nevertheless, as the article constitutes a critical reflection of my own

---

[2] See Chandler, *Brother Number One*; Short, *Pol Pot*.
[3] The notable exception is Hinton, "Why Did You Kill?"; Hinton, *Why Did They Kill?*.

ethnographic practice in the field, it juxtaposes these subjective experiences with established methodological and ethical standards.

Specifically, I encountered five key challenges during my fieldwork: (1) it was difficult to locate appropriate people to speak with as few social networks between former perpetrators exist today in many parts of the country; (2) in general, when speaking to former perpetrators, there are great incentives for the individuals to avoid honest responses as people want to disassociate themselves from their previous actions; (3) interviewing former perpetrators in some contexts leads to their stigmatization in their local communities, which would be an ethically unacceptable consequence of a researcher's intervention in the field; (4) further ethical questions arise about what to do with any potentially incriminating evidence which arises during the interview; (5) lastly, there were diverging perceptions between the interviewees and myself regarding how to categorize their role in the Khmer Rouge, with them seeing themselves as victims and my project implicitly framing them as perpetrators.

None of these challenges in the field are insurmountable, but they can be countered or at least tackled to a certain degree by choosing certain approaches to fieldwork. In this paper I discuss three types of field research, long-term stays in the community, frequent visits and building networks in the community, and repeat individual visits to select people without embedding oneself as a researcher in the community. Each of these approaches to conducting fieldwork entails specific advantages and disadvantages pertaining to how they deal with these challenges and it is the discussion of these limitations and opportunities which is the focus of this piece. Ethnographic research is well established in Cambodia and various methods which I discuss in this article have been used in research on other topics. For example, long-term, immersive stays with participant observation of the researched community have been used to study sexuality and sex work[4] and violent practices of economic dispossession in post-conflict Cambodia.[5] In-depth interviews as part of frequent visits to one and the same community, building networks here, was a research strategy for studying women's activism against land evictions.[6] The third category of targeted interviews on specific topics around different localities was employed to study rural sustainability and the negative impact of government and private sector projects on social equity and environmental safeguards.[7] It is within these various research traditions in Cambodia in which this project sought to find its methodological approach to the specific topic of perpetrators.

To this end, I will first briefly introduce the research project which provides the empirical underpinning for these methodological, conceptual and ethical

---

[4]Hoefinger, "Professional Girlfriends."
[5]Springer, *Violent Neoliberalization.*
[6]Brickell, "Intimate Geopolitics."
[7]Sokphea, "Practices and Challenges Towards Sustainability."

reflections. Next, I present the various available approaches to conducting fieldwork with former perpetrators of mass violence. Then I detail five key challenges experienced in conducting this fieldwork with former cadres of the Khmer Rouge in Cambodia and discuss how the different types of field-work approaches can provide opportunities to overcome these challenges or which are particularly susceptible to them.

Researching former cadres of the Khmer Rouge

The research project within which I conducted the field research which this article is based upon seeks to answer the question of why people participate in genocide and began conceptually by developing a model on the motivations of individual, low-level participants. The model draws on a broad range of available theoretical and experimental literature from social psychology, psy-chology, criminology, sociology, anthropology, as well as empirical case studies mostly from the Holocaust and the 1994 genocide in Rwanda. The insights from these very diverse research fields are then synthesized into what I have named the *Complexity of Evil* model.[8] The model is the most sys-tematic and schematic approach to theorizing individual perpetrators' motiv-ations for participating in genocide yet and differentiates between motivations, facilitative factors and contextual conditions.

In a second research step, the model was then tested empirically for the least-likely crucial case of the Khmer Rouge genocide in Cambodia. This test highlighted that the model, as an abstraction of empirical reality, was helpful for explaining individuals' participation across different cases. As such the empirical manifestation of the various motivations, facilitative factors and contextual conditions were quite different across the different cases but with the underlying mechanism on which the empirical manifes-tations were founded being the same for individuals in the different cases.

I will give a few more details on the model and its particulars here, as it is crucial to understand the nature of the project and of my research focus in order to understand the reflections in this article. Only by understanding my epistemological approach and the focus of my research questions, can one understand my fieldwork challenges and how I decided to deal with these in order to elicit responses which would allow me to collect the data necessary for conducting the research project.

Motivations are mechanisms which guide individuals in their choice between action alternatives, that is they are the actual impetus for acting in the way the individual ultimately does; as such they are INUS[9] conditions

---

[8]For a full version of the model see Williams, *The Complexity of Evil*; for an earlier version of the model see Williams, "The Complexity of Evil."

[9]An INUS condition is an insufficient, but necessary part of an unnecessary but sufficient condition. For the full causal implications of the concept, see Mackie, "Systematic and Nonsystematic Processing."

for participation and at least one motivation is necessary for participation to occur, although it is irrelevant which motivation(s) it is. Facilitative factors do not suffice to allow someone to participate, but they do make participation easier for the individual. Contextual conditions create the larger framework within which genocide unfolds and thus also participation occurs; these are macro-level conditions which can affect the salience or feasibility of certain motivations and facilitative factors.

The *Complexity of Evil* model identifies 11 motivations across 3 categories. The category of ingroup-focused motivations, which are based on interactions within the perpetrator group, includes individuals being motivated into participation by social influence exerted through obedience to authority, peer pressure or social conformity, as well as these relationships being laced with coercion; furthermore, individuals can take on a role and fully identify with it and its behavioural expectations. Outgroup-focused motivations are built on perceptions of the victim group and include emotions towards the victims such as fear, anger or hatred, as well as motivations by which the perpetrators are motivated to kill the victims for ideological reasons. Third, self-focused motivations are located within the perpetrators themselves and include opportunistic incentives such as career aspirations, personal or political feuds, economic gain, etc., seeking to gain status, the thrill of participation and wanting to gain sadistic pleasures.

Facilitative factors include moral justification through legitimating ideologies and euphemistic language; moral disengagement through dehumanization of the victims or social, physical and emotional distancing from the victims; the power of groups through the displacement or diffusion of responsibility in them, deindividuation and anonymity in this group and the effects of a division of labour; as well as time-sensitive factors such as desensitization over time, and the continuum of destruction and escalating commitments.

Contextual conditions are macro-level elements of the model which define the genocidal context. Here, most importantly we are talking about attributes of the state, particularly authoritarian regimes; societal tensions around ethnicity and discrimination; genocidal ideologies; political uncertainty, upheaval and war; economic factors; and various cultural factors.

The nature of the *Complexity of Evil* model is key to these methodological reflections as it frames the remit of interest in the interviews; as such, I was interested in a holistic understanding of my interviewees' perceptions at the time, including not only their own thought processes, but also perceptions of their social relations, group dynamics and the immediate and wider context they were embedded in. As such the research incorporates important insights from social psychology, sociology, but also economic reasoning and ideas about political ideologies. It is the fieldwork with former cadres of the Khmer Rouge in Cambodia which is the empirical backdrop for my reflections in the rest of this article.

Possible approaches to fieldwork with former perpetrators

In order to approach the topic of perpetrators and participation in genocide, it is necessary to speak with the individual agents of this action and to understand their perspectives on the violence and their motivations for it. This section will discuss three possible approaches to studying agents of violent conflict, each slightly different in their approach, but also each takes the idea of ethnographic fieldwork seriously, what Gearoid Millar details for international interventions as the 'recognition of the importance of culture in shaping how individuals see and experience their world and a willingness to try to understand alternative experiences'.[10] Understanding these alternative experiences is particularly important in the context of researching perpetrators as without a full understanding of their motivations, we cannot really explain the violent processes. Furthermore, perpetrator experiences will differ significantly from victim experiences, which are often privileged in research on violence as they are the objects of the horrific acts. This is problematic as the violent events will 'typically seem worse to the victim than to the perpetrator'[11] and thus to understand the perpetrators gives us a different and new perspective on the processes of violence.

The first approach to conducting fieldwork with former perpetrators is most typical to anthropology and means staying in a community for an extended period of time and immersing oneself in the local dynamics. This approach has been used in various different projects of conflict research,[12] and has sometimes been used as a method for approaching research on perpetrators. Most prominently, Alexander Laban Hinton's work on perpetrators of the Khmer Rouge in Cambodia was based on such long-term immersion in a community, although much of his research approach focused on broader cultural explanations which go beyond the individual perpetrators themselves.[13] More broadly also on perpetration and post-conflict dynamics, Eve Monique Zucker has used such an approach to study post-conflict community reconciliation,[14] Anne Yvonne Guillou to research forms of memory of the Khmer Rouge period including 'potent places' and spirits[15] and Judy Ledgerwood to explore the resilience of post-conflict social ties and village communities.[16] To a certain degree, this long-term approach can be seen as an ideal point for ethnographic research as it allows the researcher the highest degree of immersion into the context being studied and will provide some

---

[10]Millar, *Ethnographic Approach to Peacebuilding*, 6.
[11]Baumeister, "The Holocaust and the Four Roots of Evil," 243.
[12]Among many others, see Halilovich, *Places of Pain*; Menzel, *Was vom Krieg Übrig Bleibt*; Millar, *Ethnographic Approach to Peacebuilding*.
[13]Hinton, "Why Did You Kill?"; Hinton, *Why Did They Kill?*.
[14]Zucker, "Matters of Morality"; Zucker, "Trauma and Its Aftermath."
[15]Guillou, "An Alternative Memory"; Guillou, "Khmer Potent Places."
[16]Ledgerwood, "Buddhist Ritual."

of the richest insights; it is, however, extremely demanding in terms of time to be invested, language and cultural skills needed, etc.

A second possible approach, which is significantly more common in studies on perpetrators, sees researchers selecting one or multiple locations where they return to again and again and build up networks within these communities, but without actually fully embedding themselves here. A typical example of such research would be the studies by Lee Ann Fujii[17] and Erin Jessee[18] on perpetrators of the Rwandan genocide, as well as some of the biographical history conducted on the Holocaust.[19] In Cambodia, this research strategy has been gainfully implemented by Peter Manning in his work on memory and reconciliation, including the memories of perpetrators.[20] This approach is a slightly toned down version of the full anthropological approach, but retains many of its advantages, while allowing the researcher the flexibility to come and go more freely, but still getting to know the dynamics in one or more particular areas in-depth.[21]

The third approach discussed here sees people seeking out and approaching certain individuals who are of topical interest (perpetrators here) and visiting them once or several times. Some researchers will interview most respondents only once, while others will speak to them multiple times in an attempt to build up a relationship of trust and elicit more in-depth answers. This type of research has been conducted by Scott Straus,[22] Omar McDoom,[23] Alette Smeulers,[24] Kjell Anderson[25] among many others to study perpetrators across a range of different cases, as well as in Cambodia by Meng-Try Ea and Sorya Sim to study motivations for joining the Khmer Rouge,[26] Laura McGrew to analyse post-conflict community reconciliation[27] and Tallyn Gray to understand conceptions of justice and transition.[28] This type of approach allows the researcher to survey a broad range of perpetrators, from different regions, sometimes even from different countries, enabling a wider perspective on the subject. The price for this breadth comes in terms of depth and obviously such an approach means that it is not possible to trace specific social networks in one location or build up one local history.

---

[17]Fujii, *Killing Neighbours.*
[18]Jessee, *Negotiating Genocide in Rwanda*; Jessee, "Rwandan Women No More."
[19]E.g. Sereny, *Into that Darkness.*
[20]Manning, "Reconciliation and Perpetrator Memories."
[21]For a good overview of the advantages of this type of approach, see Fujii, *Killing Neighbours*, chapter 1.
[22]Straus, *The Order of Genocide.*
[23]McDoom, "The Psychology of Threat;" McDoom, "Who Killed in Rwanda's Genocide?"; McDoom, "Antisocial Capital."
[24]Smeulers, "Female Perpetrators."
[25]Anderson, *The Criminology of Genocide.*
[26]Ea and Sim, *Victims and Perpetrators?*
[27]McGrew, "Pathways to Reconciliation."
[28]Gray, *Justice and Transition.*

Finally, there are also a plethora of further ways to approach the subject of studying perpetrators more broadly, including police interrogations and court documents[29] or transcripts of clandestine audio recordings of imprisoned former perpetrators.[30] However, these will not be the focus here, but instead only approaches in which the researcher actually interacts with and can question the former perpetrators themselves, only forms of ethnographic fieldwork. Each of these approaches has been used in the past to study the question of what motivates people to become perpetrators, each resulting in different forms of data and insight; thus, no approach is inherently better than the other, but in researching perpetrators in this context, each has distinct advantages and disadvantages. These will be discussed with reference to the particular challenges of interviewing former perpetrators in the Cambodian context.

The chosen research approach

A brief overview of how I actually conducted my fieldwork is in order at this point, before then being able to reflect on this and discuss the main challenges I encountered and how I dealt with them. First, what do I even mean by the term perpetrator and by participation in the violence of the Cambodian genocide? As argued elsewhere, the utility of the idea of perpetrator is limited in that it essentializes the individual to a degree and almost ascribes the person with a characteristic; instead, it is more useful to approach this topic from an action-centric perspective which foreground the actions of individuals, allowing people to engage in different types of actions, including bystanding or resistance at different points in time.[31]

These different types of actions are understood broadly, not just as the person who actually killed, but also those people who were necessary cogs in the preceding processes, arresting, guarding and interrogating prisoners, or giving the orders for these actions. Furthermore, a broader conception of what constitutes a perpetrator is necessary in Cambodia as the essence of the genocide of the Khmer Rouge goes beyond the eradication of ethnic minorities;[32] it includes the executions of individuals associated with the former regime, as well as increasingly purges within the Khmer Rouge itself of people suspected of being traitors, as well as the killing of any person in the population acting in an anti-revolutionary manner.[33] However, going further than this, the Khmer Rouge erected a regime of such totalitarian

---

[29]Browning, *Ordinary Men*; Goldhagen, *Hitler's Willing Executioners*.
[30]Neitzel and Welzer, *Soldaten*; Welzer, *Täter*; Welzer, Neitzel and Gudehus, *"Der Führer war wieder viel zu human."*
[31]Williams, "I am Not, What I am"; see also Gudehus, "On the Significance of the Past."
[32]For an historical overview of the genocidal process in Cambodia see Chandler, *A History of Cambodia*; Kiernan, *How Pol Pot Came to Power*; Kiernan, *The Pol Pot Regime*.
[33]Chandler, *Voices from S-21*, 45–76.

magnitude that hundreds of thousands of individuals died of hunger, exhaustion and disease;[34] as such, acts of perpetration also include overseeing working groups and insisting on people working until they die, denying one's workers sufficient food, reporting on people who were not performing adequately as suspected anti-revolutionaries, etc. Violence in the context of the Cambodian genocide is more complex and nuanced and so understanding participation in it, that is motivations for engaging in acts of perpetration necessitated a holistic understanding of people's perceptions of their position and their context at the time. Thus, perpetrators are individuals who engage in an action which contributes to the overall death and killing processes which were occurring during Democratic Kampuchea.

In order to find individuals who were involved in these types of actions and thus interesting for the project, I opted for the third approach presented in the previous section, purposively selecting individual interviewees based on prior knowledge of what types of positions they had been in, altogether interviewing 58 former Khmer Rouge. Given that this was my first project in Cambodia, I was reliant on contacts through other researchers and institutions. I received contacts from my translator, a Cambodian scholar who has been researching Khmer Rouge history for several years, from the research centre and archive DC-Cam and their publications, from various NGOs who knew of former Khmer Rouge in the communities they were working in, as well as from other researchers and from chance encounters.[35] For only a few interviewees was I the first one to speak with them, but the overwhelming majority had only been interviewed once or twice before me, meaning that they were not 'practiced interviewees' with a fixed narrative;[36] I spoke only with a couple of more seasoned interviewees who had spoken to dozens of journalists, investigators and researchers. I approached people not as 'perpetrators' but as individuals who had been part of the Khmer Rouge, wanting to understand more about their experiences in the regime.

As I am not a Khmer native speaker, the interview was conducted through a translator who himself is not a professional translator but a Khmer Rouge historian; this enabled him to translate not just the content, but the significance of the meanings of what interviewees were saying, particularly when

---

[34]On detailed tabulations of victims see Tabeau and Kheam, *Demographic Expert Report.*

[35]Given that I received some of my contacts from DC-Cam, it would have been interesting to compare the responses given to me in my interviews with those in the previous interviews. However, DC-Cam's interviews focus much more on the facts of when individuals were where and in which position than on the meanings these individuals assign to their actions and their understandings of the situations they were in, which was central to my project, rendering a comparison not very constructive.

[36]Also, when I asked interviewees about their previous interview situations, the interviews often appear to be strongly biographical in nature, focussing much more on the geographical locations and structural positions the individuals were in, than their perspectives on their participation and the context they were in. This is also the case for any publicly available interviews I could find of people with whom I spoke, meaning that I cannot systematically compare there previous narratives with what they told me, as the questions posed in the interviews differ.

interviewees used metaphors and propaganda phrases from the Khmer Rouge period. The translator translated summarily rather than synchronously, so as not to distract or interrupt the interviewees in their flow; most of the interviews were recorded (although being careful to anonymize the recordings so it was not traceable who the interviewee was) and then subsequently transcribed by my research assistant. Both my assistant and I are males in our late 20s; while my translator is highly respected as he has a university degree, he himself comes from a farming family in the provinces; as a white Westerner I was perceived having a relatively high status. In this combination, my translator was able to build strong rapport, while my status as a foreigner meant I was able to ask 'obvious' or 'stupid' questions and interviewees were prepared to explain seemingly every-day or mundane stories about the Khmer Rouge period, which they felt would not have been relevant to a Cambodian who already 'understood' the way things were.

In order to gain an insight into various facets of life under the Khmer Rouge and to gradually approach the topic of violence more organically, I structured the interviews as life histories, although most of the interview was spent on discussing their life between 1970 and 1979, the period of Democratic Kampuchea and the preceding civil war. Interviewees were free to guide the direction of the interview, although I then asked more focused questions as topics of interest arose in conversation. For the most part, I was able to conduct interviews without any listeners, but when other people did join the conversation, I postponed more contentious issues for later interviews.

Dealing with challenges in interviewing Cambodian perpetrators

While seeking to understand the motivations of former cadres of the Khmer Rouge to participate in violence, a multitude of challenges arose. While challenges in accessing interviewees and conducting the interviews is normal in ethnographic research, this section will discuss the precise problems encountered in Cambodia. While part of these may be idiosyncratic to the case, I would argue that much of it will be recognizable to people studying perpetrators in other contexts. For each of the challenges, I then also discuss how the various approaches to conducting fieldwork can help solve or possibly even exacerbate these problems.

Lack of networks between interviewees

The first challenge was that it emerged during the research process that few networks between the former perpetrators exist today, as over 40 years have gone by since the Khmer Rouge took power and former cadres are dispersed across the country. Two main reasons exist why these former cadres no longer have contact to each other.

First, during the regime most cadres were relocated away from their homes and most often split up from any friends or acquaintances they were recruited with; thus, they were thrown into new social settings with people they did not know.[37] Normally, people would build up relationships quickly in such situations, however, this did not occur for these former cadres of the Khmer Rouge. The absolute dominance of *Ângkar*,[38] as the organization of the Khmer Rouge was called, and the constant search for internal enemies within the organization who were trying to undermine the revolution meant that anyone could be suspected to be an enemy. Furthermore, there were incentives for people to denounce others (whether they were enemies or not), particularly in self-study and criticism session;[39] this meant that people kept to themselves as much as possible in order not to show too much of themselves.[40]

Second, when the regime collapsed as a result of a Vietnamese invasion and in the ensuing chaos most cadres then either fled North and East with the retreating Khmer Rouge or returned to their pre-Khmer Rouge homes. Either way most people have not seen any of their former comrades since the fall of the regime as they were then located somewhere different and because there was no incentive to seek out contact with people to whom one had not built up strong ties during the regime.

While the dynamics described here are certainly particular to the Cambodian setting the consequences of these, that one is confronted with a lack of social networks between former perpetrators in most of the country, is probably not. This lack of a network between former perpetrators outside of a few former stronghold areas had methodological consequences, first, for even being able to find relevant people to speak with, and second, for being able to study social dynamics in the groups at the time from various perspectives.

If one were to select an anthropological, long-term approach within one community, one would thus have very few former perpetrators and many victims within that community, at least within social networks which knew each other. The only exception to this, are some regions on the border to Thailand which remained strongholds of the Khmer Rouge until the late 1990s,[41] but these communities tend to be quite hostile to foreign researchers

---

[37]Interview conducted by the author with a former militiaman, later also group leader, in August 2014 in Battambang province.

[38]Hinton, *Why Did They Kill?*, 132.

[39]For more details on self-study and criticism sessions see Path and Kanavou, "Converts, Not Ideologues?" 306; Thion, "Cambodian Idea of Revolution," 29.

[40]Interview conducted by the author with a former military messenger and secretary in November 2014 in Prey Veng province.

[41]Due to a lack of statistics on this topic, it is unclear how many former Khmer Rouge there are in Cambodia in total, and furthermore how many live in the former strongholds. My tentative assessment would be that those living outside the strongholds are considerably more numerous, thus resulting in most former Khmer Rouge not being embedded in such social networks.

working on the topic of the Khmer Rouge and it is unlikely one would be able to spend a considerable amount of time there and actually gain a foothold in the community. In principle, such a long-term approach would be possible for this topic, but it would be extremely challenging and time-demanding and it would be unclear if it would actually lead to fruition. Equally and for the same reasons, it is not feasible to select one or multiple locations in Cambodia to which one can frequently return in order to build up networks within these communities and map the social dynamics therein.

Thus, in order to be able to speak to different people about these issues, rather than just one or two individuals (as has also been done in past research),[42] it was necessary to conduct a series of interviews with different individuals spread across a variety of locations. In this way it was possible to tap into the experiences of various perpetrators, but was unable to tap into the broader community. For this specific project, the broader community is not really needed, although had there have been several perpetrators who were together during the Khmer Rouge period, it would certainly have provided valuable insights to discuss the same events and day-to-day life stories from their varying perspectives.

(Dis)honest responses

The second key challenge when speaking to any former perpetrators is that the incentives are stacked against eliciting honest responses. In principle it is easier for the interviewee not to admit that one has committed horrific deeds in the past than to admit to having done so.

In principle, the longer a researcher spends with the former perpetrator the more trust he or she should be able to build to the individual and thus raising the chances of an honest response. This would render an anthropological, long-term approach most tenable. However, such trust can also be built up over a longer period when visiting a person several times. One advantage that the third approach could have, where the researcher interviews just isolated, individual people, is that they do not need to worry about any of the issues they talk about being discussed in the community they live in. Of course, researchers guarantee anonymity for their interviewees, but it could be easier to speak frankly to an outsider who comes to visit only from time to time, than to engage with someone who has become a member of the community and is present permanently (at least for a certain amount of time).

An idiosyncrasy of the Cambodian case is, however, that many former perpetrators see themselves as victims and this is accepted by the majority of the population,[43] a strong contrast to other cases such as Rwanda;[44] this is

---

[42]Hinton, *Why Did They Kill?*; Zucker, "Matters of Morality"; Zucker, "Trauma and Its Aftermath."
[43]Williams, "Perpetrator-Victims."
[44]Jessee and Williams, "Perpetrators as Victims?"

primarily the case in communities in which the perpetrators were assigned to work in another part of the country, as was most often the case;[45] tensions arise and guilt is assigned primarily in communities when the perpetrator remained in their home community.[46] Even in former stronghold areas, individuals often do not present themselves as committed Khmer Rouge cadres, likewise deflecting their perpetration and sometimes employing similar appeals to victimhood as in other places. This provides a researcher of Cambodian former perpetrators with a distinct advantage as they see many of their performed actions as constituting part of their victimhood. The rationale underlying this is that they had been forced to commit these actions, many of which would typically be associated with perpetrators, such as killing, ordering killings, arresting victims, torturing, etc. Thus, these former perpetrators believed themselves to be victims for having been forced to commit these deeds. As victims, in turn, they were quite prepared to speak about these actions openly, explaining why they and other people had committed them. While the logic of them being victims was rooted in the duress that forced them to commit these actions, they did speak about a host of other motivations behind these actions, too.

Potential community stigmatization

A third potential problem of working with perpetrators of mass violence is that my presence and my focus on them could have consequences for them in their own local settings. Potentially, my interaction with them could lead to their stigmatization in the community by me being in the villages and people knowing what my research is about, particularly if their communities were previously unaware that these individuals were former perpetrators.

As highlighted above, most low-level perpetrators are seen as victims like the rest of society living at the time, according to the majority of the population, but nonetheless, if people were aware of the precise nature of their roles in the previous regime, or even of the actual people who were their victims, it is possible that these people could be seen as perpetrators and to some degree stigmatized. While most of society is content with a narrative which places the responsibility for the crimes solely with those individuals who were in the highest echelons of power, if the concrete nature of individual crimes were known about individuals who had been mistreated in this specific community, former perpetrators may be turned on.[47]

---

[45] Jessee and Williams, "Perpetrators as Victims?"

[46] See, for example, Zucker, "Trauma and Its Aftermath."

[47] While there were some revenge killings directly after the fall of Democratic Kampuchea, hostilities towards former Khmer Rouge in communities since have normally only targeted individuals who were responsible for the mistreatment of people *in that specific community*.

As such, it is certainly safer for the communities in which research on former perpetrators is being conducted not to know the nature of the research project, so that they cannot infer from the researcher's focus on certain individuals that these must be perpetrators and so that they then do not start asking questions or passing judgement. To this end, long-term anthropologic research could be more difficult, as could broad, repeat community research as both approaches would involve the whole community learning – at least in broad strokes – what the nature of the research project is. Targeted visits to specific individuals known to be of interest, on the other hand, are most likely to protect the interviewees, as the researcher does not need to interact with the rest of the community and does not need to inform them of the nature of the research project.

Incriminating evidence

A fourth challenge in conducting perpetrator research in general and Khmer Rouge research in particular is also the question of interviewees self-incriminating themselves legally through their interview testimonies. It is, thus, important to reflect on the ethical challenge of what to do with any potentially incriminating evidence which arises during the interview. This is particularly sensitive when there exist local or international tribunals which may try to access these interviews. Interviewees open up to the questions of researchers in response to promises during informed consent that their responses will be stored anonymously and not shared with others.[48] At the same time, however, tribunals can have significant interest in these testimonies either with a view to prosecuting these individuals or calling them as witnesses. In the most extreme cases, it is even possible for tribunals to not only question researchers under oath as to their sources, but also to subpoena their interview recordings, transcripts or even the contact details of their interviewees.

In Cambodia, it was very unlikely that any of the people I was speaking to would ever be tried, as they had all been low-level perpetrators; however, there were very real chances that they could be summoned as witnesses by the Extraordinary Chambers in the Courts of Cambodia (ECCC), the hybrid tribunal adjudicating the Khmer Rouge trials. For some of my interviewees this questioning in front of court would not have posed any emotional or social problems and they would have enjoyed the chance to tell their story to a broader audience and be able to participate in the trial against the genocidal leaders. As part of the ECCC proceedings, there are also civil parties who can lodge claims as victims against the defendants and several of the registered individuals are actually former low-level Khmer Rouge cadres.[49] This

---

[48]Fluehr-Lobban, "Ethics"; Höglund and Öberg, "Improving Information Gathering and Evaluation"; Wood, "The Ethical Challenges of Field Research."
[49]Bernath, "Complex Political Victims."

highlights their accepted status as victims in societal discourse and demonstrates that for some being called to testify is seen as an opportunity not a problem. However, this is also certainly not the case for all of my interviewees.

In terms of gauging which of the research approaches could be most productive in ensuring one's research subjects anonymity is upheld and any legally self-incriminating statements not pursued, it would appear that the long-term, anthropological approach is more problematic as the researcher is based solely in one area from which it becomes significantly easier to track with whom the researcher has spoken. Similarly, the second research approach is jeopardized by this, although to a lesser degree, as the researcher only comes to the community periodically. The most promising approach again would be the individual interviewee approach, as long as the researcher is careful to maintain anonymous notes only of where he or she has travelled and with whom he or she has spoken.

Diverging understandings of interviewee identity

The final challenge to interviewing perpetrators rests in diverging perceptions between the interviewees and the researcher regarding the precise identity or label to adhere to the role the interviewee played. As a researcher I am conducting a research project on former members of the Khmer Rouge as perpetrators and was trying to glean insight into their motivations for engaging in various acts of perpetration during the Khmer Rouge regime. My interviewees, on the other hand, felt themselves that they were victims of the regime, as has already been alluded to above. These two perspectives are not mutually exclusive and their self-perception of victimhood does not necessarily contradict my analytical categorization of their actions as those of perpetration. Also, as argued above, as different people can engage in different actions at different times, it is less useful to think of people as perpetrators *per se* but instead take an action-based approach and focus on the actual actions of the individuals. Thus, people can perpetrate, be bystanders, rescue and resist at different points in time, and they can also be victims, too.

These complicated narratives are pivotal to understanding how people look back on their past and to also understand how people live together today. While these can be tapped into by a targeted, interviewee by interviewee approach, the nuances of how people construct each other in a community will be more easily and richly tapped into, the more in-depth a researcher is embedded in the community. Ultimately, as a researcher I never used the concepts of perpetrators or perpetration when speaking to my interviewees, but instead focused on and remained open to their perspectives, taking any self-proclamations at face value and reserving the labelling as perpetration actions etc. for later in my subsequent analyses.

Besides these more conceptual problems, this topic is further ethically problematic, if and when the interviewees provide references to other possible interviewees with whom it could be interesting for the researcher to speak. Given the lack of networks this was seldom the case in Cambodia, but for other cases this could be more salient. This is problematic because from the perspective of the interviewee they are introducing the researcher to other victims or bystanders, but at the same time they are actually also incriminating the other person from the analytical perspective of the researcher.

The approach which can deal with these ethical problems best is again the community-based, anthropological, long-term approach or the community-centric second approach, because these will have significantly lower thresholds for people introducing the researcher to other people. If the researcher interacts with people on a day-to-day basis, there is less onus put on referrals to other people and less weight afforded to what this might mean, given that the researcher is embedded in regular relations with people across the communities anyway.

Conclusion

This article has presented various challenges which researchers can experience during fieldwork conducted with former perpetrators of mass violence and has reflected on how the various approaches to ethnographic fieldwork interact with these challenges, sometimes amplifying them, but other times successfully moderating them. The three forms of ethnographic fieldwork which I focused on in this piece were long-term anthropological forms of immersing oneself in a community as a researcher, regular and in-depth visits to a community and, lastly, repeat visits to individual interviewees without interaction with the rest of the community. The rest of this piece then discussed the drawbacks and advantages of these various types of ethnographic fieldwork for five distinct issues of working on the topic of perpetrators, referring back to my own research project which saw me interviewing former cadres of the Khmer Rouge in various locations across Cambodia: the lack of networks between former perpetrators in Cambodia due to their social isolation under the regime and their chaotic return to their homes in the downfall of the regime; the veracity of responses; the potential for interviewees to be stigmatized in their communities; the question of what to do with incriminating evidence; the ethical issue of diverging perceptions of perpetration and victimhood between interviewees and the researcher.

This paper cannot and does not want to provide a definitive answer on which form of ethnographic field research is better, nor what the best way to deal with each one is. Each of these approaches – and several more – have been used productively for research in Cambodia and elsewhere and each bring with them various advantages. Instead this article has aimed solely at providing a tentative reflection of the opportunities each approach provides and the limitations inherent to them, particularly in the context of my own research on former cadres of the Khmer Rouge. The methodological choices which I made were directed by the context of my specific project; this paper is, thus, not an endorsement of a specific approach but a reflection of methodological and ethical issues which can come up when researching perpetrators and a discussion for this one context. Despite the idiosyncrasies of my project on perpetrators and the Cambodian case, other researchers should be able to take some of these thoughts and use them to reflect on their own research practices, too.

Possibly the best approach to ethnographic fieldwork could be to 'mix and match' these approaches. In the end, such sensitive research as that of speaking with the perpetrators of mass violence, can be expected to bring significant challenges with it, and only by reflecting on these during and after the process of fieldwork, can we speak to and evaluate the limitations of our role in the field and gauge how we can improve our practices in gathering data, crucial for answering these types of research questions.

Acknowledgements

I am grateful for the comments of the two anonymous reviewers, as well as the editor Gearoid Millar.

Disclosure statement

No potential conflict of interest was reported by the author.

Bibliography

Anderson, Kjell. *The Criminology of Genocide: Killing Without Consequence.* London: Routledge, 2016.
Baumeister, Roy F. "The Holocaust and the Four Roots of Evil." In *Understanding Genocide. The Social Psychology of the Holocaust*, eds Leonard S. Newman and Ralph Erber, 241–58. Oxford: Oxford University Press, 2002.

Bernath, Julie. "'Complex Political Victims' in the Aftermath of Mass Atrocity: Reflections on the Khmer Rouge Tribunal in Cambodia." *International Journal of Transitional Justice* 10 (2016): 46–66.

Brickell, Katherine. "'The Whole World is Watching': Intimate Geopolitics of Forced Eviction and Women's Activism in Cambodia." *Annals of the Association of American Geographers* 104 (2014): 1256–72.

Browning, Christopher. *Ordinary Men: Reserve Police Battalion 101 and the Final Solution in Poland.* New York: Harper Collins, 1994.

Chandler, David. *Brother Number One. A Political Biography of Pol Pot.* Boulder, CO: Westview, 1999.

Chandler, David. *Voices from S-21. Terror and History in Pol Pot's Secret Prison.* Chiang Mai: Silkworm, 2000.

Chandler, David. *A History of Cambodia.* 4th ed. Boulder, CO: Westview, 2008.

Ea, Meng-Try, and Sorya Sim. *Victims and Perpetrators? Testimony of Young Khmer Rouge Comrades.* Phnom Penh: Documentation Center of Cambodia, 2001.

Fluehr-Lobban, Carolyn. "Ethics." In *Handbook of Methods in Cultural Anthropology*, eds H. Russell Bernard and Clarence C. Gravlee, 131–150. London: Rowman & Littlefield, 2015.

Fujii, Lee Ann. *Killing Neighbours: Networks of Violence in Rwanda.* Ithaca, NY: Cornell University Press, 2009.

Goldhagen, Daniel Jonah. *Hitler's Willing Executioners. Ordinary Germans and the Holocaust.* London: Abacus, 1996.

Gray, Tallyn. *Justice and Transition in Cambodia 1979–2014: Process, Meaning and Narrative.* PhD thesis. London: University of Westminster, 2014.

Gudehus, Christian. "On the Significance of the Past for Present and Future Action." In *Theorizing Social Memories: Concepts and Context*, eds Gerd Sebald and Jan Wagle, 84–97. London: Routledge, 2016.

Guillou, Anne Yvonne. "An Alternative Memory of the Khmer Rouge Genocide: The Dead of the Mass Graves and the Land Guardian Spirits [*neak ta*]." *South East Asia Research* 20 (2012): 207–26.

Guillou, Anne Yvonne. "Khmer Potent Places. A Localised Idea of Royalty, Buddhism and Ancestrality." *Kyoto Review of Southeast Asia* 20 (2016), https://kyotoreview.org/issue-20/embodied-memory-cambodia/.

Halilovich, Hariz. *Places of Pain. Forced Displacement, Popular Memory and Trans-Local Identities in Bosnian War-Torn Communities.* New York: Berghahn, 2013.

Hinton, Alexander Laban. "Why Did You Kill? The Cambodian Genocide and the Dark Side of Face and Honor." In *Violence in War and Peace. An Anthology*, eds Nancy Scheper-Hughes and Philippe Bourgois, 157–68. Malden: Blackwell, 2003.

Hinton, Alexander Laban. *Why Did They Kill? Cambodia in the Shadow of Genocide.* Berkeley: University of California Press, 2005.

Hoefinger, Heidi. "Professional Girlfriends. An Ethnography of Sexuality, Solidarity and Subculture in Cambodia." *Cultural Studies* 25 (2011): 244–66.

Höglund, Kristine, and Magnus Öberg. "Improving Information Gathering and Evaluation." In *Understanding Peace Research: Methods and Challenges*, eds Kristine Höglund and Magnus Öberg, 185–98. London: Routledge, 2011.

Jessee, Erin. *Negotiating Genocide in Rwanda: The Politics of History.* New York: Palgrave Macmillan, 2017.

Jessee, Erin. "Rwandan Women No More: Female Génocidaires in the Aftermath of the 1994 Rwandan Genocide." *Conflict and Society* 1 (2015): 60–80.

Jessee, Erin, and Timothy Williams. "Perpetrators as Victims?" forthcoming.

Kiernan, Ben. *How Pol Pot Came to Power. A History of Communism in Kampuchea, 1930–1975.* London: Verso, 1985.

Kiernan, Ben. *The Pol Pot Regime. Race, Power, and Genocide in Cambodia under the Khmer Rouge.* New Haven, CT: Yale University Press, 1996.

Ledgerwood, Judy. "Buddhist Ritual and the Reordering of Social Relations in Cambodia." *South East Asia Research* 20 (2012): 191–206.

Mackie, D. M. "Systematic and Nonsystematic Processing of Majority and Minority Persuasive Communications." *Journal of Personality and Social Psychology* 53 (1987): 41–52.

Manning, Peter. "Reconciliation and Perpetrator Memories in Cambodia." *International Journal of Transitional Justice* 9 (2015): 386–406.

McDoom, Omar. "The Psychology of Threat in Intergroup Conflict: Emotions, Rationality, and Opportunity in the Rwandan Genocide." *International Security* 37 (2012): 119–55.

McDoom, Omar. "Who Killed in Rwanda's Genocide? Micro-space, Social Influence and Individual Participation in Intergroup Violence." *Journal of Peace Research* 50 (2013): 453–67.

McDoom, Omar. "Antisocial Capital: A Profile of Rwandan Genocide Perpetrators' Social Networks." *Journal of Conflict Resolution* 58 (2014): 865–93.

McGrew, Laura. "Pathways to Reconciliation in Cambodia." *Peace Review* 23 (2011): 514–21.

Menzel, Anne. *Was vom Krieg Übrig Bleibt: Unfriedliche Beziehungen in Sierra Leone.* Bielefeld: transcript, 2015.

Millar, Gearoid. *An Ethnographic Approach to Peacebuilding. Understanding Local Experiences in Transitional States.* Abingdon: Routledge, 2014.

Neitzel, Sönke, and Harald Welzer. *Soldaten. Protokolle vom Kämpfen, Töten und Sterben.* Frankfurt am Main: S. Fischer, 2011.

Path, Kosal, and Angeliki Kanavou. "Converts, Not Ideologues? The Khmer Rouge Practice of Thought Reform in Cambodia, 1975–1978." *Journal of Political Ideologies* 20 (2015): 304–32.

Sereny, Gitta. *Into that Darkness. 'The Mind of a Mass Murderer'.* London: Picador, 1974.

Short, Philip. *Pol Pot. A History of a Nightmare.* New York: Henry Holt, 2005.

Smeulers, Alette. "Female Perpetrators: Ordinary or Extra-ordinary Women?" *International Criminal Law Review* 15 (2015): 207–53.

Sokphea, Young. "Practices and Challenges Towards Sustainability in Cambodia." In *The Handbook of Contemporary Cambodia*, eds Katherine Brickell and Simon Springer, 111–22. Abingdon: Routledge, 2017.

Springer, Simon. *Violent Neoliberalism. Development, Discourse, and Dispossession in Cambodia.* New York: Palgrave Macmillan, 2015.

Straus, Scott. *The Order of Genocide: Race, Power, and War in Rwanda.* Ithaca, NY: Cornell University Press, 2006.

Tabeau, Ewa, and They Kheam. *Demographic Expert Report: The Khmer Rouge Victims in Cambodia, April 1975 – January 1979. A Critical Assessment of Major Estimates.* Phnom Penh: Extraordinary Chambers in the Courts of Cambodia (ECCC), 2009.

Thion, Serge. "The Cambodian Idea of Revolution." In *Revolution and Its Aftermath in Kampuchea. Eight Essays*, eds David Chandler and Ben Kiernan, 10–33. New Haven: Yale University Southeast Asia Studies, 1983.

Welzer, Harald. *Täter. Wie aus ganz normalen Menschen Massenmörder werden.* 2nd edn. Frankfurt: S. Fischer Verlag, 2006.

Welzer, Harald, Sönke Neitzel, and Christian Gudehus. *'Der Führer war wieder viel zu human, viel zu gefühlvoll'. Der Zweite Weltkrieg aus der Sicht deutscher und italienischer Soldaten.* Frankfurt: S. Fischer, 2011.

Williams, Timothy. "Perpetrator-Victims. How Universal Victimhood in Cambodia Impacts Dealing with the Past and Transitional Justice Measures." In *Understanding the Age of Transitional Justice: Narratives in Historical Perspective,* ed Nanci Adler, forthcoming.

Williams, Timothy. "'I Am Not, What I Am.' A Typological Approach to Individual (In)action in the Holocaust." In *Probing the Limits of Categorization: The Bystander in Holocaust History,* eds Christina Morina and Krijn Thijs. New York: Berghahn, 2017.

Williams, Timothy. *The Complexity of Evil. Modelling Perpetration in Genocide.* Marburg: PhD thesis at Centre for Conflict Studies, Marburg University, 2017.

Williams, Timothy. "The Complexity of Evil: A Multi-Faceted Approach to Genocide Perpetration." *Zeitschrift für Friedens- und Konfliktforschung* 3 (2014): 71–98.

Wood, Elisabeth Jean. "The Ethical Challenges of Field Research in Conflict Zones." *Qualitative Sociology* 29 (2006): 373–86.

Zucker, Eve Monique. "Matters of Morality: The Case of a Former Khmer Rouge Village Chief." *Anthropology and Humanism* 34 (2009): 31–40.

Zucker, Eve Monique. "Trauma and Its Aftermath: Local Configurations of Reconciliation in Cambodia and the Khmer Rouge Tribunal." *The Journal of Asian Studies* 72 (2013): 793–800.

With Soymilk to the Khmer Rouge: Challenges of Researching Ex-combatants in Post-war Contexts

Anne Hennings

ABSTRACT
This contribution suggests how to identify and deal with ex-combatants in (un)peaceful post-war environments from a methodological perspective. While it is obvious that large-N studies or standardized interviews fall too short to depict post-war dynamics and related conflict risks, ethnographic methods face numerous challenges, too. First, the identification of and access to former combatants may prove to be difficult. Often being stigmatized or perceived as outlaws they may not wish to get in touch with 'outsiders', like academics. Second, researchers need to be careful not to worsen the status of ex-combatants and at the same time make sure to maintain a trustful relationship with the rest of the community. Moreover, certain ethics apply when addressing sensitive war or contemporary issues (e.g. land grabs), even more, if there is a lack of amnesty. I aim at critically discussing questions of trust, legitimacy, networks, the necessity of 'going local', as well as logistics that can exacerbate dealing with ex-combatants or even pose a threat to researchers. Before concluding, I briefly delineate dilemmas related to the researcher's role and her responsibility for field assistants. The article largely draws on my extensive ethnographic fieldwork experience in Cambodia and ethnographic literature on (post-)war settings.

Introduction

[My research assistant] and I arrive with a six-pack of soymilk at a house in Malai town right on the Thai border in the early morning. The sun is yet to become merciless but for now bathes the lush green garden and the dew above the stream in golden light. What a welcoming change to the dry land we passed by in Battambang province, land that suffers from heavy deforestation and this year's severe drought. Accompanied by twittering birds and the purling stream we approach a well-laid picnic table in the middle of this beautiful, almost picturesque, setting that takes me aback. Who would expect such an extraordinary and warm welcome at the house of one of the leading intellectuals of the Khmer Rouge?

(Excerpt from my field notes, July 2016)

Prior to my arrival in Cambodia, I was wondering, and to a certain degree worried, about whether and how I would get access to former Khmer Rouge cadres and soldiers. Whilst some concerns proved valid, as in the former stronghold of Anlong Veng, the task turned out to be easier than expected when I approached high-ranking cadres in other longstanding strongholds, such as 'Brilliant Number 2' whom I visited in the setting described above. He worked closely with Ieng Sary, in the Ministry of Foreign Affairs of Democratic Kampuchea in the 1970s and was co-responsible for the post-war land redistribution in the stronghold of Malai. The situation was different though outside the Khmer Rouge strongholds, where I approached rural communities composed of former low-ranking Khmer Rouge soldiers, refugees or Internally Displaced Persons, and villagers originating from the area. As identifying ex-combatants[1] was key to my research, I had to find some way to do this that did not undermine reconciliation processes or cause intra-community conflicts by digging up the past. But how do you identify and deal with ex-combatants without the risk of your interlocutors losing face?

This article takes a closer look at the challenges and ways of dealing with ex-combatants in sensitive post-war contexts. Given the number of researchers in post-conflict countries the void in the literature regarding this issue seems quite surprising. Indeed, there are several publications on how to conduct (ethnographic) research in conflict zones,[2] or even practical guides for personal safety in these contexts.[3] Some of this literature might likewise apply to post-war and peace research, like Wood who outlines various aspects that may challenge the ethical imperative in (post-) war environments: 'Political polarization, [...] the unpredictability of events, and the traumatization through violence of combatants and civilians alike.'[4] Nonetheless, the vulnerability of peace processes and societies in transition calls for specific considerations and do no harm measures.[5] In response, Millar recently introduced what he calls Ethnographic Peace Research (EPR), an umbrella approach for researchers and practitioners in sensitive post-conflict settings who explore the impact of peacebuilding interventions or dynamics of reconciliation and conflict transformation.[6] Based on four pillars – the experiential lens, local engagement, ethnographic preparation, and reflection on one's individual implicit assumptions – EPR allows the researcher to unpack local experiences and concepts, such as those of justice, healing, security, or empowerment.[7]

---

[1]Ex-combatants include former rebels, militia, or paramilitary members among others. That said, I am aware that in some cases it may be difficult to distinguish them.
[2]Wood, "The Ethical Challenges of Field Research"; Brun, "'I Love My Soldier'".
[3]Mazurana and Gale, "Preparing for Research in Active Conflict Zones".
[4]Wood, "The Ethical Challenges of Field Research," 373.
[5]Anderson, Do No Harm.
[6]Millar, An Ethnographic Approach to Peacebuilding.
[7]Ibid., 61.

My research focuses on analysing the micro-politics of contestation against land grabbing in post-conflict settings and its potential repercussions on conflict transformation. The contemporary land rush for agriculture, mining, or carbon trading purposes, to name but a few, plays out particularly in the Global South.[8] In recent years, much has been written on the various impacts of large-scale land deals and growing attention paid to the emergence of contestation.[9] Yet, the consequences for countries coming to terms after years of war that face challenges of return and recovery remain underexplored.[10] My emphasis on ex-combatants will serve as a lens to uncover potential risks of land grabbing for peace and stability in post-conflict environments. Since land has always been important to the Khmer Rouge, from a spiritual, territorial, and livelihood perspective, I was interested in whether and to what extent they would react to land grabbing in a certain way. Which means of contestation do they choose? Would they take up arms again? With these questions in mind, I needed to gain a deeper understanding of the contemporary Khmer Rouge culture, their motivation, and the scope of the high- and low-ranking ex-Khmer Rouge's networks. In doing so, I was aware of the challenges. As Edwards put it:

> Fieldwork is always and inevitably an exercise in hope over experience, the hope being that you can pass through the barrier of culture and language to feel and understand what the world looks like for someone from some place else, which experience tells you rarely if ever happens.[11]

Using political ethnography during my 12 months of fieldwork in Cambodia in 2016/2017 was a natural choice, as it allows the researcher to explore various kinds of power, from formal to informal up to 'globalized webs of influence, dependence, and assistance'.[12] It 'invites the researcher to "see" differently; heterogeneity, causal complexity, dynamism, contingency, and informality come to the fore'.[13] Likewise, it is well suited to study collective action and (grassroots) mobilization.[14] Marcus even suggests that political ethnography should primarily focus on people leveraged by political and economic globalization dynamics who struggle with socio-economic and cultural transformation.[15] Likewise, encouraged by my conceptual assemblage perspective that, in a nutshell, entails a theory of practices and interaction, my method repertoire included non-structured interviews, dialogues, informal discussions and participatory

[8]Wolford et al., "Governing Global Land Deals"; White et al., "The New Enclosures".
[9]Hall et al., "Resistance, Acquiescence or Incorporation?".
[10]Elhawary and Pantuliano, "Land Issues in Post-conflict Return and Recovery".
[11]Edwards, "Counterinsurgency as a Cultural System".
[12]Kubik, "Ethnography of Politics," 44.
[13]Schatz, "Ethnographic Immersion and the Study of Politics," 11.
[14]Kubik, "Ethnography of Politics"; Blee and Currier, "How Local Social Movement Groups Handle".
[15]Marcus, Ethnography Through Thick and Thin, 85.

observation with NGO and UN staff, monks, officials, activists, and communities affected by land grabbing, including former Khmer Rouge. The resulting data allowed me to ponder the motivations and strategies of everyday resistance, overt advocacy politics, and official resistance. In this contribution, however, I only focus on my ethnographic experience with the former Khmer Rouge.

The article starts out with Cambodia's recent conflict history and the contemporary political situation, followed by an overview of relevant groups of ex-Khmer Rouge in terms of their rank and spatial location. In the following two sections, I then discuss the challenges of identifying and accessing former rebels and closely related issues of trust building and renewed stigmatization. The last part of the article offers some reflection on the researcher's role, the sympathies at play, and points out challenges for research assistants.

The research context: the former Khmer Rouge in northwestern Cambodia

Genocide, civil war, trauma, and increasing repression

Much has been written about Cambodia's troubled history and the spillover effect of the Vietnam war in the 1960s, which is why I will outline the cornerstones only briefly. By 1970, when the US-backed General Lon Nol staged a military coup against Prince Sihanouk, the Pol Pot-led Khmer Rouge – supported by China – had turned already into an armed guerilla movement. Following Mao's ideas, they captured Phnom Penh in 1975, proclaimed 'Year Zero' and controlled the fate of Cambodia for almost four years; a 'period of deliberate murder, starvation and overwork in which approximately 1.7 million people [about a quarter of Cambodia's population] died'.[16] Ousted by the Vietnamese army in 1979, the Khmer Rouge dispersed into the forested western borderlands, where they continued fighting and engaged in illegal timber and jade trade to finance their struggle.[17] Being now a government in exile (the Khmer Rouge represented Cambodia officially in the UN until 1993 as part of a tripartite exile government), the Khmer Rouge cadres reorganized and increasingly recruited and mobilized soldiers in the refugee camps along the Thai border. The liberation through the Vietnamese army was followed by what most Cambodian's describe as a decade-long occupation by their 'arch-enemy', Vietnam, and former Khmer Rouge soldiers who had defected earlier. The civil war between royalists, communists, anti-Vietnamese groups, and the government, largely supported by Vietnamese

---

[16]Clarke, "Research for Empowerment in a Divided Cambodia," 93.
[17]However, other warring factions including Vietnam likewise used that strategy. Gottesman, *After the Khmer Rouge*, 157.

troops, lasted almost another decade and came only briefly to a halt after the
Paris Peace Accords were signed in October 1991. After long negotiations, the
Khmer Rouge in Malai and Pailin gave in eventually in 1995, whilst the last
stronghold Anlong Veng followed only three years later.[18] In 2003, the UN
and the Cambodian government agreed to establish the Extraordinary
Chambers in the Courts of Cambodia (ECCC) to try high-ranking senior
leaders of the Khmer Rouge for alleged crimes during the Khmer Rouge
regime.

Over 30 years of civil war, genocide, forced displacement, and the experience of loss have led to social disruption and left a traumatized Cambodian
society behind. One day, expressing my discontent about the prevalent distrust among Cambodians, a colleague put it straight: 'Part of our communi-
cation culture has been destroyed during the Khmer Rouge time and the
war. We lost trust in each other. Not trusting anyone or speaking up was a
survival strategy, you know.' Different experiences and interpretations have
furthermore led to social division, particularly along the (thin) line between
victims and perpetrators. As Clarke put it, 'In Cambodia, ethnicity, language,
religion do not divide: history does.'[19] Accordingly, decade-long political
instability and large-scale violence still tear at the social fabric and challenge
efforts to rebuild trust.[20] Other scholars, in contrast, question whether social
cohesion has ever existed in the first place. Notably, Frings observed that
'when Cambodians do help they always try to take some advantage from it
[...]. [They] don't think they have a moral obligation [to help]'.[21] Kim
would not go that far. He argues that patterns of social interaction are
largely restored, although he adds that urbanization and monetarization challenge the rebuilding of trust and solidarity.[22] Whilst I agree that intra-community trust has increased, my findings show, in line with Kim, that
mistrust prevails *between* communities, further amplified by land grabbing.
Instead of supporting the Cambodian society to regain trust at large, the
ruling CPP under Prime Minister Hun Sen, who has been in power since
the early 1980s, keeps instrumentalizing the Khmer Rouge revolution and
their atrocities to sow fear and strengthen his own power. The message is
clear: We have saved you and if we fall, the country will return to violence,
terror, and darkness again. In doing so, Hun Sen has created a climate in
which silencing is a common method to repress critical voices and prevent
political change.

Last year, on the 25th anniversary of the Paris Peace Accords, UN special
rapporteur Rhona Smith emphasized that many of its elements 'are not yet

---

[18]However, fighting continued in some places on a smaller scale until the early 2000s.
[19]Ibid., 92.
[20]Simon Springer, *Cambodia's Neoliberal Order*, 50.
[21]Frings, "Cambodia after Decollectivization 1989–92," 61.
[22]Sedara, "Reciprocity," 153–4, 168.

fully fulfilled', raising especially concerns about the upcoming elections, unresolved land conflicts, and related violations of human rights.[23] This environment leaves only limited space for research on collective action or land grabbing and raised a number of safety concerns for research participants and myself.[24] Increasing restrictions on freedom of expression and assembly and a society scared of new violence makes it difficult to address people in public settings. As I will illustrate later, I managed to research mostly 'under the radar', whilst my interlocutors were under the microscope. Despite the associated risks, many Cambodians allowed me insights into their practices of coping and contention and shared even sensitive information.

By region, rank, and degree of reintegration: the former Khmer Rouge today

Nowadays, ex-Khmer Rouge cadres and soldiers can generally be distinguished in one of two ways: First, according to their spatial location within or outside the strongholds, and second, in terms of their position during the genocide and/or civil war. For me as a researcher, it was highly important to acknowledge the characteristics and lived realities of these groups to be able to approach them accordingly. Considering the level of reintegration and the vulnerability to land conflicts, I first outline the inside–outside stronghold axes before looking at the privileges or pitfalls that result from their respective positions.

After the Khmer Rouge were expelled by Vietnamese troops, most took refuge in the forests along the Thai border. However, over the course of the civil war they were only able to maintain three strongholds, namely Pailin, Malai, and Anlong Veng. Each of them exhibit distinct features that are reflected in their relation to the government and internal hierarchies. Former Khmer Rouge in Malai and Pailin laid down their arms in 1995 and have established close ties with the government. In interviews, high-ranking cadres in these areas described how Hun Sen himself tried to persuade them to join the CPP and his government – an invitation a number of them accepted for pragmatic reasons. Hun Sen's appeasement strategy, some speak of a win–win policy, was simple. He promised land, prestigious positions in the government, immunity,[25] and a level of political autonomy in the strongholds if they abandoned the guerilla war. The last stronghold,

---

[23]Baliga and Chheng, "UN Envoy Says Paris Peace Accords".

[24]See also Beban and Schoenberger, "They Turn Us into Criminals"; Brun, "'I Love My Soldier'," 13 on creating save spaces in Sri Lanka.

[25]However, the ECCC later refused to recognize the Royal Decree that granted high-ranking cadres amnesty, as its scope excluded serious international crimes allegedly committed during the 1970s. See Ciorciari and Heindel, "Experiments in International Criminal Justice," 388.

Anlong Veng, on the other hand, disapproved of what was going on under Ieng Sary's leadership in Malai and Pailin, and was reluctant to give in until 1998. The strongholds have long since reconciled and former high-ranking cadres maintain good relationships for the most part. After defection, the cadres in Anlong Veng, too, benefited from high positions (especially in the military), as well as a certain amount of autonomy over land and local authorities. Nevertheless, high-ranking Khmer Rouge in Anlong Veng have remained rather exclusive and suspicious of outsiders.

Hun Sen's concessions, and the conveniences that come along with them, are probably the main reason why most high-ranking cadres and their off-spring still live in the former strongholds. Most of these senior military, political, or intellectual figures are quite well-off today. In interviews, older cadres were up-to-date, not only about developments in Cambodia, but in the world. It was obvious that some of them have tried to come to peace with the(ir) past. For example, some generals or intellectuals I met became devoutly Buddhists or Christians, others wanted to pass their stories on to Cambodians and foreigners.

Whilst many of the old cadres reside in the relative safety of Malai, Pailin, and Anlong Veng (or Phnom Penh, if they joined the government), many low-ranking ex-soldiers either went in search of employment to Thailand or live in impoverished conditions in northwestern Cambodia. Moreover, there are numerous mid-ranking Khmer Rouge who made good in local or provincial politics. In the early 1980s, various ex-Khmer Rouge were appointed to leading positions in local authorities, simply because many old leaders were killed during the genocide. Hughes et al. found that many local authorities across Cambodia have practically remained in power since then, 'dominated by a static highly politicized and male leadership group'.[26] In contrast to the low-ranking soldiers, these ex-Khmer Rouge could retain power and increase their sphere of influence. On the other hand, simple 'foot soldiers' lack influential networks to this day. Whilst often well integrated in mixed communities outside the strongholds, they remain exposed to the 'perpetrator-discourse' though most joined the Khmer Rouge only after 1979.

Apart from political and military positions, allocating land turned out to be a pivotal appeasement strategy both inside and outside the strongholds. But the land redistribution processes for each varied across these geographies. Whilst the 'first come first served' principle dominated in Anlong Veng, despite the Khmer Rouge's ideological fundament of agrarian socialism, land was fairly equally distributed in Malai and Pailin, with each family receiving about five hectares. This contrasts strongly with experiences of lower-ranking ex-Khmer Rouge soldiers outside the strongholds, who either

---

[26]Hughes et al., "Local Leaders and Big Business in Three Communes," 254.

received much smaller plots from the government or, in most cases, simply settled down anywhere.[27] Needless to say, subsistence farming for them was rather a question of survival and less of ideology.

Interestingly, up to today the government – being afraid of renewed mobilization – has not enforced any economic concessions in the strongholds even though much of the land would be suitable for agricultural investment. Yet, the situation is totally different for ex-Khmer Rouge outside the strongholds. Many low-ranking soldiers in mixed communities have already been evicted or lost their farmland due to land grabbing. In Kampong Speu and Kampot provinces, whole former divisions are confronted with large-scale investments and displacement. The combination of being a former low-ranking Khmer Rouge and living outside the strongholds poses numerous challenges for land grab-affected communities. In addition to having poor capacities and less influential networks, they can hardly show solidarity with ex-comrades under the watchful eye of the suspicious government who would immediately repress any hints of a potential uprising. Ironically, I also came upon land conflicts between former low-ranking and high-level Khmer Rouge, who hold provincial government or military positions outside the strongholds. In these cases, the government not only seems to be even more reluctant to intervene but also to have its hands tied, as high-level Khmer Rouge networks are still very influential.

Identifying and accessing ex-combatants and related questions of do no harm

With all of the associated risks, one might question the necessity of approaching ex-combatants a decade or two after the end of a war. Indeed, most post-war research focuses on what Marten's calls the 'peace-kept' with emphasis on survivors and 'victims'.[28] Despite its importance, only a few surveys or evaluations measure the long-term impact of reintegration projects, the general socio-economic well-being of former combatants, or the potential of (new) conflict risks. Whilst the field of ex-combatant studies remains underexamined, scant attention has been paid to questions of how to deal with and interview victims of war and genocide. In both cases, however, the researcher needs to be aware of her own footprint, and its potential threat to conflict transformation and local reconciliation processes. In short, the effort to identify 'who is who' within the local requires tact, intuition, and efforts to build trust. Among the Khmer Rouge, for example, there is a strong wish for unity in spite of certain cultural features in the strongholds. Low- and high-ranking Khmer Rouge alike kept emphasizing that one cannot say Khmer

---

[27]Most Khmer Rouge soldiers could opt between a small plot of land, educational training, or money.
[28]Marten, *Enforcing the Peace*.

Rouge or non-Khmer Rouge. Especially, if it comes to land conflicts or political repression they underline the 'We are one, we are Khmer'-narrative. Also, it is ethically highly problematic to differentiate societies simply along the victim–perpetrator axis.[29] As Menzel argues, black and white classifications of (un-)peaceful post-conflict societies fall too short to mirror complex and nonlinear dynamics during war times and following years.[30] Thus, like in any research setting, one needs to be sure to speak to various subgroups, for example, in and outside the former strongholds, including ex-combatants of different age, rank, and gender. In this section, I discuss the ethical challenges that evolve around identifying and accessing ex-combatants.

'Have you fought for the Khmer Rouge?'

As mentioned before, talking to former Khmer Rouge, and hence identifying them in the first place, was important to my research. Depending on how peace was achieved, a question about someone's revolutionary background might be enthusiastically answered in certain post-conflict contexts. Particularly, when it comes to deeply ideologically rooted guerilla groups that take a certain pride in their ex-rebel identity, or if ex-combatants could maintain a certain status quo, and/or were granted amnesty.[31] In contrast, interlocutors might refuse to talk or the conversation may only touch the surface if they fear prosecution. In Cambodia, especially high-ranking cadres were suspicious of potential ECCC undercover investigators who used to pretend to be researchers or NGO staff. Whereas I never witness this practice myself, not only former Khmer Rouge but also acquaintances working at the ECCC told me about it under the quiet.

In Cambodia almost 20 years on, the reaction to questions regarding one's Khmer Rouge background varies depending on the (spatial) context and the person's former position. For example, posing it in one of the former strongholds might be perceived as rather naïve; it is a matter of course that almost every man or woman from a certain age on has supported the Khmer Rouge directly or indirectly.[32] Yet, asking this blunt question in a group setting of a mixed community will most likely cause fear and shame. Although most villagers roughly know about their neighbours' past, interlocutors could lose face when admitting that he or she was a Khmer Rouge soldier and may once again be stigmatized as a perpetrator – no matter for what reasons they joined or were forced to join. Obviously, communities in northwestern Cambodia outside the strongholds are very concerned and protective when it comes to

---

[29]Mani, *Beyond Retribution*, 123.
[30]Menzel, *Was vom Krieg übrig bleibt*, 39.
[31]Wood, "The Ethical Challenges of Field Research," 378.
[32]Although this changes slowly, as more and more migrants from other parts of Cambodia seek income opportunities and open small businesses in the former strongholds.

retaining their social cohesion. After years of war and recurrent displacement, most communities had no choice but to live together and support each other as a matter of survival. Accordingly, they would not disclose war-related identities to outsiders easily though representatives might provide this information if they trust the researcher and she creates a safe space. Recognizing and respecting these boundaries should be of the highest priority, however important it may be to identify interviewees for one's studies.

Research 'can be very intrusive and may profoundly disturb the local social fabric'.[33] Reflecting on her research in post-genocide Rwanda, Thomson emphasizes the researcher's responsibility 'to protect the physical, social and emotional wellbeing of the people she researches in ways that respect their individual rights'.[34] Whilst taking this into account, two strategies proved to be of great help. First of all, I gathered as much information as possible about a certain community, for example, by getting in touch with local NGOs, researchers or, if available, research institutes working in this area. These people are usually very knowledgeable and, once they trust you, are happy to share insights. However, this strategy is in most cases only well suited to identify higher ranks or contemporary community representatives, which is why it can only be a starting point. Second, trust building and spending time in the communities – as shall be discussed – remains pivotal both to identify and access ex-combatants.

Seeking access: issues of affiliation, logistics, and research permits

Once identified, access to former combatants still might prove difficult and poses several challenges. In this section, I will address challenges of physical access, the risk of renewed stigmatization, and the pros and cons of research permits. In many post-war environments, researchers face numerous logistical challenges, for example, they may be physically denied access to land mine-affected areas or turned down at military checkpoints. Northwestern Cambodia is not only heavily mined but also highly militarized since the latest Thai border conflict that was settled in 2011. At the same time, local authorities have increasingly set up road blocks in order to monitor and limit movement to land conflict-affected areas. In these cases, I was either forced to travel on hidden paths, cancel the meeting last-minute, or – if possible – meet interlocutors at a safer place, for example, in a small nearby town.

Besides that, ex-combatants may not wish to get in touch with 'outsiders', like academics, as they fear renewed stigmatization or undercover investigations. Differences between accessing high- or low-ranking Khmer Rouge became obvious at an early stage of my research. Especially low-ranking

---

[33]Susan Thomson, "Academic Integrity and Ethical Responsibilities in Post-Genocide Rwanda," 148.
[34]Ibid.

Khmer Rouge, who take an active part in resisting land grabbing and are closely monitored and threatened by the military, tended to be more hesitant. It took lots of patience and networking to meet these communities. If they finally agreed, we usually met in secret places, for example, in my hotel room or in the rice fields. In sharp contrast, access to high-ranking Khmer Rouge in the strongholds, who are mostly still in charge and less bothered by government (land) policies, turned out to be easier – except for Anlong Veng. It is usually assumed that once you are on good terms with key actors of your target group, the snowball principle will do the rest, but in my case I could not simply reach out to cadres in other strongholds due to the fragmented nature of the Khmer Rouge leadership. Discussing challenges of access, other researchers kept telling me that they encountered problems when they refused to pay high-level cadres they intended to interview, but I was never asked to do so. In short, the expectations of ex-combatants towards researchers may vary significantly, depending on their former rank and contemporary position, and the researcher's background and networks.

Being affiliated to the Phnom Penh-based Heinrich Boell Foundation turned out to be quite advantageous. In most remote areas, the foundation was not known but appreciated as a German institution. In the end, it was a researcher of the Documentation Center of Cambodia (DC-CAM), the key institution on Khmer Rouge studies, who brought me in touch with some high-ranking cadres in Anlong Veng and Malai, such as 'Brilliant Number 2'. To my advantage, the former Khmer Rouge intellectuals and comman-ders I talked to mostly respected and trusted DC-CAM.[35] Researchers usually find themselves in less official webs of local affiliations, including NGOs, which facilitate entry to certain communities, share personal phone numbers of officials or ex-Khmer Rouge cadres, provide (secure and reliable) transport, or even shelter. Besides the obvious benefits, this can be problematic in two ways. First, those networks may be perceived as partial and should be chosen carefully as the researcher may become easily entangled in power relations an outsider can never fully grasp.[36] Second, hosts may restrict the researcher's interactions and travel.[37] Yet, a lack of accommodation or sometimes the need to be courteous, may require the researcher to accept an offer to stay. On the other hand, staying in an ex-combatant community or at the house of a high-ranking cadre offers the researcher excellent trust building opportunities and allows insights into (everyday) practices and power dynamics. Ethnographic peace researchers must be aware of these pros and cons which may be key to the success of the research project. It is helpful to put out a few feelers in the

---

[35]This does not mean, they agreed with all of DC-CAM's research findings.
[36]Brun, "'I Love My Soldier'," 130.
[37]Wood, "The Ethical Challenges of Field Research," 379.

beginning to see whether certain networks or NGOs are appreciated or trusted before disclosing one's affiliations.

In many post-war contexts, ex-combatants often retain a distant and rather difficult relationship to the authorities. Accordingly, anecdotal evidence shows that obtaining a research permit can be a decisive – but often under-estimated – factor for accessing ex-combatants successfully. For example, research permits can nurture distrust or be interpreted as joining hands with the government. In Cambodia, an official permit – if issued at all – often means closer monitoring by the authorities and, in turn, more attention to the communities the researcher works with. This poses a threat especially to low-ranking Khmer Rouge who take over leading positions in organizing and mobilizing villagers against land grabbing. On the other hand, high-ranking Khmer Rouge tend to require official permissions, as they fear prosecution by the ECCC. I heard of a researcher who had to turn around, travel 400 km back to Phnom Penh to get the document, and was only then allowed to talk to them. After long discussions with fellow researchers, and due to the highly sensitive nature of my research project, I eventually opted against an authoritative permission to the benefit of do no harm. Instead, I always carried a letter of reference from the Boell Foundation with me. Additionally, local NGO staff were eager to give advice about how to best explain my presence to the military which occasionally stopped me. Nonetheless, I never felt comfortable telling military officials that I was interested in the local culture or ecosystem whilst traveling to remote villages, where the forest was long gone and there were no indigenous people around. In the end, it proved to be a wise decision to not obtain a permit. Being part of a network trusted by the high-ranking Khmer Rouge I met gave me sufficient credibility that allowed me to approach them. In short, before obtaining an official authorization researchers in (post-) conflict zones always should care-fully consider the overall political situation, the socio-political status of former combatants, and their own safety.

Building trust in an insecure environment

In any research context, building trust with participants is pivotal to gain access to information and for security reasons. Yet, it proves to be a difficult task for researchers in disrupted post-conflict or post-genocide societies.[38] Interlocutors may perceive the research topic to be too dangerous, it may cause old sores to reopen or even violent reactions. Where there is a general lack of trust, participants, and particularly ex-combatants, have much to lose by exposing sensitive or too much information. It may also be a balancing act to primarily approach ex-combatants whilst maintaining a

---

[38]See also Norman, "Got Trust?".

trustful relationship with the rest of the community. At the same time, researchers may be at risk in a 'violent society', as Clarke and her team experienced in early post-war Cambodia.[39] So how can one gain trust researching sensitive issues after decades of war and violence? This is only more challenging, in an increasingly repressive context like contemporary Cambodia, where '[...] not only the elderly still have the feeling angka is watching'.[40]

During my fieldwork, I identified three major factors that helped me to build a trustful relationship with ex-combatants, which I will discuss in the following. First, I outline how researchers can gain legitimacy through their networks and take advantage of their own personal background. Second, I illustrate the relevance of ensuring confidentiality and, lastly, point out challenges of 'going local' with ex-combatants.

The quest for legitimacy

The researcher's legitimacy depends on various more or less given factors, such as the researcher's attitude, origin, age, or gender, which I will outline in the following. It goes without saying, that showing respect and appreciation provides the basis for building trust. Hence, as a 'cultural outsider', I carefully prepared my field trips by discussing current developments, hierarchies, and specific features with other researchers, local NGO staff, or neighbouring communities. In so doing, I also gave thought to appropriate gifts or tokens of appreciation. Whilst I usually brought food, drinks, fruits, and so on, to the villages, I was genuinely uncertain about what is suitable for the aged Khmer Rouge elite. Finally, just before the meeting I describe at the outset, a moto taxi driver gave me a hint: Soymilk would do it. Still sceptical, my translator and I arrived with a six-pack of soymilk in this picturesque setting depicted in the introduction. It might sound surprising that soymilk can open doors to aged cadres, but our host was genuinely pleased. Most high-ranking Khmer Rouge have maintained a very disciplined lifestyle and live up to the 12 moral principles of the Khmer Rouge. Interviewees emphasized that they abstain from excessive drinking, gambling, or women, in contrast to their offspring whose lifestyle they often disapprove. They rather keep themselves physically and mentally fit, value hospitality and honesty, and take care of their health. For this reason, 'Brilliant Number 2' and his fellows appreciated the soymilk as a thoughtful present.

When using ethnographic methods, it is often details that facilitate trust and foster relationships. As such, I made use of my Eastern German origin when introducing myself to the benefit of my legitimacy. This was for two reasons. First of all, most high- and low-ranking Khmer Rouge received

---

[39]Clarke, "Research for Empowerment in a Divided Cambodia," 102.
[40]Interview with Om Chariya (TPO), May 27, 2016.

reintegration support from the German Konrad Adenauer Foundation from the mid-1990s to the early 2000s, which is why Germans are still well recognized in this area. Second, being born in socialist German Democratic Republic naturally established common ground with my interlocutors and implied a particular knowledge or experience. After talking about my origin with one retired General, for example, he declared: 'The Khmer Rouge dream in silence. But if someone is interested like you are, we can share and tell.' In addition, being based in northwestern Battambang and not the capital, where most expats, researchers, and NGO people live, also opened doors. Giving up the comfort of Phnom Penh implicated genuine interest in the Cambodian culture and their struggle. Although I still did not live 'next door' to most communities, interviewees expressed they felt as if they could reach out to me any time. It turned out that living in the region made it also easier to catch up over mutual acquaintances; an important asset in a kinship and network-based society.

Besides personal characteristics and one's origin, gender and age can enhance or foreclose access to certain information. As a female researcher in her late twenties, I was unsure if the former Khmer Rouge would accept me – most of them being my parents or grandparents age. Moreover, according to their point of view women are considered inferior and thus, should not be involved in politics (or research). In fact, during my field trips I met very few – but exceptionally strong – female representatives, mostly outside the strongholds. Whilst one ex-Khmer Rouge was only appointed because of her literacy, another gained her credibility from being a widow of a high-ranking cadre. Except for these few women, former Khmer Rouge communities are still very much organized and represented by men. A nephew of Pol Pot and now retired General made his opinion about (Khmer) women very clear: 'We are the same. But you know, their comprehension and thinking is not like a man's. She just follows orders.' As a European woman, I was always respected and trusted by men and women of all ages and could engage in genuine discussion with aged cadres and low-ranking Khmer Rouge alike. I was probably viewed less as a threat to them than a male researcher might had been. I was surprised, in fact, to not be lectured at or seen as incapable or unsophisticated as Vorrath experienced researching political elites in Burundi.[41] This might be closely related to the fact that I behaved rather like a 'man' according to Cambodian norms, for example, by traveling extensively on my own.[42] To compensate for my age, gender, and limited knowledge of the area a second field assistant,[43] in addition to my translator, accompanied me in the very beginning. Well into his seventies,

---

[41]Vorrath, "Challenges of Interviewing Political Elites," 67.
[42]See Brun, "'I Love My Soldier'," 137–8 on her experience in Sri Lanka.
[43]Yet, traveling with two field assistants goes along with numerous challenges related to age and gender differences, but also varying experiences of war and violence. See Hennings, "A Buddhist, a Christian and a Hindu on the Road."

he was widely known in northwest Cambodia and guaranteed that low-ranking ex-Khmer Rouge and other resisting villagers would trust me. That said, well-connected, impartial field assistants are not always available to researchers in post-conflict zones. Other than that, it is helpful to identify key factors that enhance one's legitimacy and, in a next step, to emphasize these; be it one's origin, expertise, or through a field assistant. In this way, the researcher may even compensate for certain given disadvantageous factors, such as age or gender.

Ensuring confidentiality in post-conflict contexts

One of my main concerns revolved around how to ensure confidentiality and consent in an increasingly repressive political environment and a lack of amnesty for ex-combatants. For security reasons, I decided to refrain from recording any interviews and discussions (even if interlocutors might have agreed to do so). Obviously, it made both low- and high-ranking Khmer Rouge also feel more comfortable, as interviews seemed less formal and they did not have to fear any consequences in case the recordings fell into the wrong hands. Whilst high-ranking cadres were concerned to jeopardize their advantageous relation to the government, low-ranking soldiers mostly feared the reaction of the military or powerful people in the government involved in the land grab. These risks in mind, I made sure to hide my hand-written notes before passing military or police checkpoints. Most of my notes contained sensitive information 'that might have political impli-cations if in the wrong hands',[44] ranging from political preferences and expressed solidarity, up to indications of covert membership in local move-ments or involvement in collective action. Although numerous Khmer Rouge cadres were integrated into the government and the military, the auth-orities keep an eye on ex-combatants, especially in the context of land con-flicts. If former Khmer Rouge join hands, the government would immediately intervene. Any joint action, even if nonviolent and based on democratic principles, would be labelled as an attempt by the Khmer Rouge to return to power. This exemplifies why confidentiality in post-war contexts must be of highest importance; even if sometimes 'the best safe space we can make is staying away'.[45]

Once a researcher sees interlocutors as participants, not subjects – which lies at the core of ethnographic research – they have the right to determine if and how the information will be used.[46] As any written document would connect the participants to the research project and could do great harm, and many low-ranking ex-combatants in rural areas are semi-literate, oral

---

[44]Wood, "The Ethical Challenges of Field Research," 381.
[45]Brun, "'I Love My Soldier'," 146.
[46]Clarke, "Research for Empowerment in a Divided Cambodia," 102.

consent often becomes a natural choice. As in any research context, it is the researcher's responsibility to guarantee the protection of sensitive data; participants can opt out at any time, and may skip certain questions. This allows ex-combatants to control the conversation and prevent them from feeling leveraged into revealing their involvement in war or other crimes. However, this participatory practice may lead to confusion in the first place. In contrast to Wood's experience of El Salvadorian residents who 'took skillful advantage of different levels of confidentiality',[47] ex-combatants in Cambodia in most cases simply agreed. This might indicate a high level of trust but it more likely hints at asymmetrical power relations between the researcher and the participants in a strictly hierarchically organized society. As such, I had to carefully weigh which material to publish, even if ex-combatants deliberately rejected anonymity.

Challenges of 'going local' with ex-combatants

Even if the researcher and her project are legitimized and confidentiality is ensured, 'going local' remains a challenge. When researching ex-combatants, the question arises even more, how much immersion is necessary, appropriate, and ethical. Whereas Millar argues that EPR detaches from standardized data collection methods but does not necessarily require one to 'go native', immersion remains a key feature of political ethnography according to Schatz.[48] He argues that immersion enables the researcher to study perceptions of justice and freedom, as they take the individual experience into account.[49] Yet, spending time with participants, just 'being there', proves to be particularly challenging in post-conflict zones. For instance, local authorities or the military may prevent or interrupt get-together of ex-combatants on the ground of renewed risks of mobilization. During my field trips to low-ranking Khmer Rouge communities that were affected by land deals outside the strongholds, I was at times secretly followed by the military or police and forced at gunpoint to leave immediately in the middle of an interview. In contrast to Brun's suggestion to 'make sure I have time to sit down with the people',[50] I was often in a rush involuntarily. Surprisingly, the tightening grip of the government and my commitment to still meet the communities in secrecy, raised sympathy and facilitated trust. Consequently, ex-Khmer Rouge were eager to provide insights into contested post-war land redistribution processes or took me to the rice fields they kept replanting despite all risks. Although I had only limited time, some shared detailed stories about the origins of the land spirits they believe in, such as Som who provided fleeing

---

[47]Wood, "The Ethical Challenges of Field Research," 381.
[48]Schatz uses immersion and participant observation interchangeably. Ibid., 5.
[49]Schatz, "Ethnographic Immersion and the Study of Politics," 10.
[50]Brun, "'I Love My Soldier'," 136.

Khmer Rouge soldiers refuge in her forest after the Vietnamese invasion in 1979 and later punished the soldiers when they heavily mined the area. In the strongholds, on the other hand, it was much easier to immerse. I spent many hours discussing world and domestic politics with high-ranking cadres and intellectuals or watched popular – highly commercialized – Thai soaps till late at night. My experience with the ex-Khmer Rouge shows that 'going local' is very much a question of spending quality time, particularly if external factors exacerbate extended stays.

Similar to other research settings, language barriers or one's timing may further impede immersion in post-war societies. Speaking the language – even if only at a beginner level – often naturally increases one's legitimacy. However, most ethnographic peace researchers spend limited time in the field or may find themselves in a setting with multiple local languages. Unlike Millar, I always felt language fluency would have allowed me to get even more intimate insights into the experiences and motivations of ex-combatants and the webs of their social networks.[51] In addition, the timing of one's presence at the research site is of great importance, though it is often external events that may alter a situation.[52] After the assassination of well-respected analyst and activist Kem Ley in mid-2016, for example, Cambodia was literally stirred up and people discussed politics openly all over the country. During the following weeks, I found myself in risky situations more than once, for example, when interlocutors accused the current government of being involved in the assassination or publicly committed to not vote for the ruling CPP again. Sometimes, I even had to call a halt to an interview for security reasons when the conversation took place at a food stall or on a bus. For many ex-Khmer Rouge, Kem Ley was a key political figure on the rise. Some even drew parallels to Pol Pot's extraordinary leadership qualities. Moreover, Kem Ley's 2015-founded Grassroots Democratic Party is well perceived in the western strongholds. Interestingly, this indicates a shift as the Malai's and Pailin's loyalty to the ruling party was unquestioned since Hun Sen's win–win policy. Yet, after Kem Ley's assassination cadres openly talked about their changing political preferences. Therefore, contingencies can help the researcher to immerse (more deeply) into the life of her target group, especially in highly politicized contexts.

Researching ex-combatants: sympathies, prejudices, and other dilemmas

This section illustrates dilemmas that researchers and research assistants may face when dealing with ex-combatants in post-conflict environments. Some

---

[51] Millar, *An Ethnographic Approach to Peacebuilding*, 6.
[52] Schatz, "Ethnographic Immersion and the Study of Politics," 11.

dilemmas, of course, do have their parallels in any research setting, like questions of reciprocation or of knowledge production and power relations. Yet, these challenges are aggravated in post-conflict contexts.[53] On the one hand, ethnographic research enables new ways of seeing and producing knowledge to the benefit of academia and the society. On the other hand, it is the (ethnographic) researcher's responsibility to be particularly sensitive to the repercussions of one's presence on local knowledge production. Researchers challenge the contemporary and 'often hegemonic categories of practice and analysis' in various ways.[54] For example, discussing questions of mobilization, (non-)violent action, and solidarity can encourage interlocutors to re-assess their current situation and capacities. It might also encourage them to push their claims in a more determined or even confrontational way, which can enhance the likelihood of violence with long-term effects on peace and stability.[55]

Likewise, EPR exposes researchers and assistants to sometimes difficult or dangerous environments, and confronts them with struggles and worldviews they may oppose or sympathize with, depending on their own background. During my fieldwork, it was obvious that at least some participants were involved in or responsible for 'some dark chapters'[56] in Cambodia's history of violence. This may cause uneasiness, reservation, or even fear among researchers and assistants. Especially translators may feel uncomfortable, as they directly talk to the ex-combatants and deal with their unfiltered emotions. Yet, the research team should refrain from judging their interlocutors. During our first fieldtrip to the strongholds, I sensed how difficult this task was for my research assistant, whose family, like most Cambodians, had suffered under the Khmer Rouge regime. When asked by two cadres where he lived, my assistant frankly said, 'close to the killing fields, you know, in the south of Phnom Penh'. Apparently, he wanted to test their reaction (there was none, at least not visibly). Throughout the interview he remained polite and chatty and expressed interest in their stories. When I encouraged him to reflect on his feelings later on, he told me that he now better understands the political and historical circumstances that led to the Khmer Rouge revolution and that he considers it important to also listen to their view on history.[57] It should be clear now that researchers in post-conflict or post-genocide contexts need to be sensitive to their research assistant's background to avoid mental stress and awkward, potentially face-losing situations. Furthermore, regular reflection on the research process, including the emotional component of approaching ex-rebels and potential perpetrators,

---

[53]Millar, *An Ethnographic Approach to Peacebuilding*, 124.
[54]Schatz, "Ethnographic Immersion and the Study of Politics," 15.
[55]See also Clarke, "Research for Empowerment in a Divided Cambodia," 97.
[56]Vorrath, "Challenges of Interviewing Political Elites," 68.
[57]Although DC-CAM and the Ministry of Education work on it, the Khmer Rouge regime and the following civil war are only about to be integrated into Cambodian school curricula.

may even offer a starting point for local research assistants to deal with the, often little-known, past of their country.

Working under extreme circumstances, ethnographic peace researchers also face numerous risks, ranging from crime or violence to lacking health and transport infrastructure. As Mertus notes:

> Researchers working in difficult situations are often a self-sacrificing and even reckless lot. They work long hours, travel across insecure borders, shrug off sexual harassment and other forms of mistreatment that they would never tolerate back home, expose themselves to incurable diseases.[58]

In terms of world views, I mostly struggled with prevalent nationalism, racism, and gender stereotypes. Yet, being confronted with contrasting concepts reminds the researcher to frequently question and critique one's own implicit assumptions, which is essential to EPR.

Being faced with post-war deprivation or marginalization naturally raises questions of how one can give back to respective communities, which remains a continuous discomfort for most researchers. I share the uneasy feeling of not being able to adequately reciprocate hospitality, time, and security risks that people take.[59] Often, low-ranking ex-Khmer Rouge asked me to function as a 'transfer gate',[60] that is, to spread the word about their land conflict case to the media, (international) NGOs, and domestic policy-makers. In contrast, high-ranking Khmer Rouge in the strongholds never asked me to do so. Whilst less affected by land conflicts, they, apparently, preferred to use their own channels and networks. In low-ranking Khmer Rouge or mixed communities, I moreover tried to reciprocate in minor ways. At times, I shared strategies and challenges of various land conflict-affected communities across Cambodia and other countries – thereby always maintaining confidentiality. In Phnom Penh, I lobbied for development projects tailored to the needs of impoverished low-ranking ex-Khmer Rouge in remote areas. Many interlocutors, however, appreciated my efforts to travel that far to discuss their issues and views. Maybe, as Wood noted, being an engaged listener to the stories others share is one sort of service a researcher can provide.[61]

Conclusion

This article outlines the challenges and dilemmas one faces when researching (activist) ex-combatants in vulnerable post-conflict contexts. Some of these issues might come up in any research setting though most are certainly

---

[58]Mertus, "Maintenance of Personal Security," 165–6.
[59]Wood, "The Ethical Challenges of Field Research in Conflict Zones," 382.
[60]Ansoms, "Dislodging Power Structures in Rural Rwanda," 50.
[61]Wood, "The Ethical Challenges of Field Research in Conflict Zones," 382.

intensified in societies of transition. My purpose here was not to develop specific guidelines for respective ethnographic research projects. Instead, I aimed to share my experience and highlight certain factors that may help researchers to cope with insecurity, distrust, or immersion, and at the same time to prevent the risk of social friction in the researched post-war society. I first provided an overview of the research context and various characteristics of Khmer Rouge subgroups in contemporary Cambodia. Next, I discussed issues that emerged around identifying and accessing ex-combatants, including logistical questions. I then illustrated how to build trust, gain legitimacy, and 'go local', all of which are even bigger challenges if interlocutors fear prosecution and/or play an active role in resisting land acquisitions. Finally, I illustrated dilemmas researchers and their assistants face, such as worldviews they may oppose or sympathize with, questions of reciprocation, and, of course, the interplay of knowledge production, power relations, and associated responsibilities.

My findings may be beneficial for evaluators who assess long-term processes of ex-combatant reintegration or for researchers who explore circumstances of re-mobilization. After all, both need to approach former rebels or paramilitaries to find valid answers. The contribution suggests that intuition and ethics must be integral to this kind of sensitive fieldwork in post-conflict zones. This means, for example, to not expose ex-combatants nor judge their 'perpetrator history', and to respect topics that are off-limits. In addition, the researcher likewise needs to take care not to pressure a community that is already under stress or put the (local) peace at risk for the sake of one's research findings, however 'groundbreaking' they might be. Moreover, I showed that engaging research assistants comes along with certain practical and ethical challenges, but also responsibilities. Ethically sound and responsible research is also about honestly acknowledging the risks and trying to keep participants and oneself safe. It requires comprehensive knowledge of the field, well-considered networks, self-reflexivity, and being up-do-date with a potentially fast-changing research context.

Acknowledgements

Helpful comments and assistance from the two anonymous reviewers and the editor are gratefully acknowledged. Moreover, the author is particularly grateful to her Cambodian research assistant. Special thanks go to her interlocutors for their hospitality and willingness to share insights as well as to her local friends and numerous supporters who largely contributed to make this research possible. All shortcomings remain author's own.

Disclosure statement

No potential conflict of interest was reported by the author.

Funding

The author would also like to thank the Heinrich Boell Foundation in Cambodia for their invaluable support as well as the German Academic Exchange Service for the field research grant.

Bibliography

Anderson, Mary B. *Do no Harm: How aid Can Support Peace-or War.* Boulder, CO: L. Rienner, 1999.

Ansoms, An. "Dislodging Power Structures in Rural Rwanda: From 'Disaster Tourist' to 'Transfer Gate'." In *Emotional and Ethical Challenges for Field Research in Africa*, ed. Susan Thomson, An Ansoms, and Jude Murison, 42–56. London: Palgrave Macmillan, 2013.

Baliga, Ananth, and Niem Chheng. "UN Envoy Says Paris Peace Accords 'Not Yet Fully Fulfilled in Cambodia'." *Phnom Penh Post*, October 20, 2016. www. phnompenhpost.com/national/un-envoy-says-paris-peace-accords-not-yet-fully-fulfilled-cambodia.

Beban, Alice, and Laura Schoenberger. "What is Academic Research on the Cambodian Frontier?" *Critical Asian Studies* (2017). doi:10.1080/14672715.2017. 1339446.

Blee, Kathleen M., and Ashley Currier. "How Local Social Movement Groups Handle a Presidential Election." *Qualitative Sociology* 29, no. 3 (2006): 261–80.

Brun, Cathrine. "'I Love My Soldier' Developing Responsible and Ethically Sound Research Strategies in a Militarized Society." In *Research Methods in Conflict Settings*, ed. Jacobsen Mazurana, Dyan Mazurana, Karen Jacobsen, and Lacey A. Gale, 128–48. Cambridge: Cambridge University Press, 2013.

Ciorciari, John D., and Anne Heindel. "Experiments in International Criminal Justice: Lessons from the Khmer Rouge Tribunal." *Michigan Journal of International Law* 35, no. 2 (2014): 369–442.

Clarke, Helen. "Research for Empowerment in a Divided Cambodia." In *Researching Violently Divided Societies: Ethical and Methodological Issues*, ed. Marie Smyth and Gillian Robinson, 92–105. Tokyo and London: United Nations University Press and Pluto Press, 2001.

Edwards, David B. "Counterinsurgency as a Cultural System." *Small Wars Journal* (2010), 1–19. http://smallwarsjournal.com/jrnl/art/counterinsurgency-as-a-cultural-system.

Elhawary, Samir, and Sara Pantuliano. "Land Issues in Post-conflict Return and Recovery." In *Land and Post-conflict Peacebuilding*, ed. Jon D. Unruh and Rhodri Williams, 115–20. London: Routledge, 2013.

Frings, K. V. "Cambodia after Decollectivization 1989–92." *Journal of Contemporary Asia* 24, no. 1 (1994): 49–66.

Gottesman, Evan. *After the Khmer Rouge: Inside the Politics of Nation Building.* New Haven: Yale University Press, 2004.

Hall, Ruth, Marc Edelman, Saturnino M. Borras, Ian Scoones, Ben White, and Wendy Wolford. "Resistance, Acquiescence or Incorporation? An Introduction to Land Grabbing and Political Reactions 'from Below'." *The Journal of Peasant Studies* 42, nos 3–4 (2015): 467–88. doi:10.1080/03066150.2015.1036746.

Hennings, Anne. "A Buddhist, a Christian and a Hindu on the Road: Lessons Learned from an Unusual Fieldtrip to the Cambodian Borderlands." In *The Challenges Undisclosed. Reflections on Invisible Experiences of Doctoral Fieldwork*, ed. Liz Storer, and Anna Shoemaker, 26–29. Field Diary Series Issue 2: Real Project, 2017. http://www.real-project.eu/wp-content/uploads/2017/03/field-diary.pdf

Hughes, Caroline, Eng Netra, Thon Vimealea, Ou Sivhuoch, and Ly Tem. "Local Leaders and Big Business in Three Communes." In *Cambodia's Economic Transformation*, ed. Caroline Hughes and Kheang Un, 245–65. NIAS studies in Asian topics 49. Copenhagen: Nias Press, 2011.

Interview with Om Chariya (TPO). May 27, 2016.

Kubik, Jan. "Ethnography of Politics: Foundations, Applications, Prospects." In *Political Ethnography*, ed. Edward Schatz, 25–52. Chicago: The University of Chicago Press, 2009.

Mani, Rama. *Beyond Retribution: Seeking Justice in the Shadows of War.* Cambridge and Malden: Polity Press and Blackwell Publishers, 2002.

Marcus, George E. *Ethnography Through Thick and Thin.* Princeton, NJ: Princeton University Press, 1998.

Marten, Kimberly Z. *Enforcing the Peace: Learning from the Imperial Past.* New York: Columbia University Press, 2004.

Mazurana, Dyan, and Lacey A. Gale. "Preparing for Research in Active Conflict Zones: Practical Considerations for Personal Safety." In *2013 - Research Methods in Conflict Settings*, ed. Jacobsen Mazurana, Dyan Mazurana, Karen Jacobsen, and Lacey A. Gale, 277–92. Cambridge: Cambridge University Press, 2013.

Menzel, Anne. *Was vom Krieg übrig bleibt: Unfriedliche Beziehungen in Sierra Leone.* Kultur und soziale Praxis. Bielefeld: transcript, 2015.

Mertus, Julie. "Maintenance of Personal Security: Ethical and Operational Issues." In *Surviving Field Research*, ed. Chandra L. Sriram, Olga Martin-Ortega, John C. King, Julie A. Mertus, and Johanna Herman, 165–76. Abingdon: Routledge, 2009.

Millar, Gearoid. *An Ethnographic Approach to Peacebuilding: Understanding Local Experiences in Transitional States.* Abingdon: Routledge, 2014.

Norman, Julie. "Got Trust? The Challenge of Gaining Access in Conflict Zones." In *Surviving Field Research*, ed. Chandra L. Sriram, Olga Martin-Ortega, John C. King, Julie A. Mertus, and Johanna Herman, 71–90. Abingdon: Routledge, 2009.

Schatz, Edward. "Ethnographic Immersion and the Study of Politics." In *Political Ethnography*, ed. Edward Schatz, 25–52. Chicago: The University of Chicago Press, 2009.

Sedara, Kim. "Reciprocity: Informal Patterns of Social Interaction in a Cambodian Village." In *Anthropology and Community in Cambodia: Reflections on the Work of May Ebihara*, ed. John A. Marston, 153–69. Monash papers on Southeast Asia no. 70. Caulfield: Monash University Press, 2011.

Springer, Simon. *Cambodia's Neoliberal Order: Violence, Authoritarianism, and the Contestation of Public Space.* Routledge Pacific Rim geographies 8. Milton Park, Abingdon: Routledge, 2010.

Thomson, Susan. "Academic Integrity and Ethical Responsibilities in Post-Genocide Rwanda: Working with Research Ethics Boards to Prepare for Fieldwork with 'Human Subjects'." In *Emotional and Ethical Challenges for Field Research in Africa,* ed. Susan Thomson, An Ansoms, and Jude Murison, 139–54. London: Palgrave Macmillan, 2013.

Vorrath, Judith. "Challenges of Interviewing Political Elites: A View from the Top in Post-War Burundi." In *Emotional and Ethical Challenges for Field Research in Africa,* ed. Susan Thomson, An Ansoms, and Jude Murison, 57–69. London: Palgrave Macmillan, 2013.

White, Ben, Saturnino M. Borras Jr., Ruth Hall, Ian Scoones, and Wendy Wolford. "The New Enclosures: Critical Perspectives on Corporate Land Deals." *Journal of Peasant Studies* 39, nos 3–4 (2012): 619–47. doi:10.1080/03066150.2012.691879.

Wolford, Wendy, Saturnino M. Borras, Ruth Hall, Ian Scoones, and Benjamin White. "Governing Global Land Deals: The Role of the State in the Rush for Land." *Development and Change* 44, no. 2 (2013): 189–210.

Wood, Elisabeth J. "The Ethical Challenges of Field Research in Conflict Zones." *Qualitative Sociology* 29, no. 3 (2006): 373–86.

Ethnographic Peace Research: The Underappreciated Benefits of Long-term Fieldwork

Gearoid Millar

ABSTRACT

While Peace Studies has always incorporated different research methodologies, large-N quantitative methods and state-level findings have dominated the literature and had most influence on policy and practice. Today, however, the limitations of peace interventions are commonly identified with the institutional, state-centric, and technocratic approaches associated with such limited understandings and their resultant policies. This paper argues, therefore, that the inability of these methods to examine local experiences of conflict, transition, and peace in diverse sociocultural settings contributes to inadequate policy formation and, thus, to problematic interventions. Indeed, the recent 'local turn' and its focus on the everyday, resistance, hybridity, and friction demands research that can better interpret local *experiences* of conflict, transition, and peace and, thereby, discover more locally salient practice. While this paper argues that an Ethnographic Peace Research (EPR) agenda must be central to such efforts, it also argues against applying the ethnographic label to work that is more suitably described as qualitative (site visits, interviews, focus groups, etc.). The paper argues that long-term fieldwork and close engagement with the subjects of peacebuilding must be required within any EPR agenda. The underappreciated benefits of such fieldwork are illustrated with examples from research in northern Sierra Leone.

Introduction

Peace Studies (PS) has experienced expansive growth in the post-Cold War period, which has paralleled the explosion of peace interventions (peace-making, peacekeeping, and peacebuilding) in conflict-affected and post-conflict societies.[1] Over this time, peace intervention by the UN and other supranational organizations gained impetus, garnered support and funding from states and their bi-lateral development agencies, and became one of the primary purposes of international society.[2] In turn, this influx of resources – today amounting to billions of dollars per year – led to strident demands for the evaluation of peace

---

[1] Jakobson, "Transformation of United Nations".
[2] Paris, "International Peacebuilding"; Tschirgi and de Coning, "Ensuring Sustainable Peace".

interventions and their impacts; new demands, in short, to evidence the beneficial effects of peace intervention.[3]

However, as supranational and civil society organizations (CSOs) developed guidelines for Monitoring and Evaluation (M&E),[4] and scholars studied the impacts of peace interventions, such assessment has become dominated by quantitative approaches and state-level research based on metrics, questionnaires, and national-level statistics.[5] The very drive for simplified, standardized, technocratic, and institutional solutions have pervaded the methods used to understand intervention.[6] This paper instead emphasizes the importance of Ethnographic Peace Research (EPR) for understanding 'local experiences', or how 'beneficiaries' of peace interventions feel about, respond to, and deal with specific interventionary mechanisms. This approach defines 'the local' variably, depending on the individuals and communities targeted by the intervention, and recognizes that the expectations of local actors prior to the intervention, and the experiences of that intervention once it has begun, may be diverse, complex, and highly contingent.

Such an approach is consistent with the critiques of peace interventions and their failure to recognize the complex sociocultural, political, and economic environments into which they intervene.[7] Such critiques note the hybrid results of peace interventions and some argue, in fact, that such interventions will inherently have unpredictable impacts.[8] As such, recent scholarship on 'friction' argues that such interventions stimulate processes of adoption, adaptation, cooptation, resistance, or rejection on the part of local actors,[9] and the impacts of intervention must, therefore, be recognized as emergent; generated in the articulation of global, national, and local institutions and actors with a range of incentives and motivations, both well-meaning and otherwise.

However, quantitative methodologies analysing state-level data cannot assess such emergent outcomes, and it is for this reason that an EPR approach, which can provide a more locally grounded perspective, is necessary. More specifically, this article will argue that EPR must assess the local experiences of peace interventions and whether and to what extent those experiences diverge from the impacts expected by international intervenors. As this article will illustrate with examples from fieldwork in Sierra Leone, such an understanding requires more than qualitative methods as often used in PS today; it requires long-term fieldwork which can provide a nuanced

---

[3]Paffenholz and Spurk, "Civil Society, Civil Engagement"; Blum, "Improving Peacebuilding Evaluation".
[4]Catholic Relief Services, "GAIN Peacebuilding Indicators"; UN, "Monitoring Peace Consolidation"; OECD, "Evaluating Peacebuilding Activities".
[5]Millar, *Ethnographic Approach*, 15.
[6]Mac Ginty, "Peacekeeping and Data".
[7]Mac Ginty and Richmond, "Local Turn".
[8]Chandler, "Peacebuilding and the Politics"; Millar, "Respecting Complexity".
[9]Björkdahl and Höglund, "Precarious Peacebuilding", 294.

understanding of the sociocultural context. It is only with sufficient time in the setting that a researcher can come to understand the situated concepts which underpin experiences of conflict, transition, and peace in post-conflict societies, and it is only by understanding these concepts that we can assess both local expectations for and the local experiences of peace intervention.

This paper is divided into four sections. The first reviews the growth of the peacebuilding field, its dominant liberal model of intervention, common methods of evaluation, and recent critiques which have focused our attention on local experiences of peace interventions. The second section explores the relationship between ethnographic fieldwork within Anthropology and an EPR agenda requiring long-term fieldwork which necessarily borrows from but cannot imitate directly the Anthropological approach. The third section discusses three key benefits of long-term fieldwork which I believe are largely underappreciated in PS scholarship. These are labelled simply as *time, chance,* and *change,* and the benefits of each are illustrated with examples from fieldwork in northern Sierra Leone. The conclusion summarizes the argument and reaffirms the key points.

The rise and critique of liberal peacebuilding

The initial post-Cold War period witnessed an incredible expansion in peace-making, peacekeeping, and peacebuilding activity as the proxy wars became more open to international intervention and the end of the veto-based neutering of the Security Council allowed the UN a more robust role in peace interventions.[10] The end of the Cold War also meant that tensions previously held in check by the balance of power flamed into outright conflict when this balance failed.[11] This was the case in the former Yugoslavia, for example, and in the former Soviet territories in the Caucuses. Similarly, new conflicts sparked in West Africa and the Great Lakes region, driven by the new economic incentives of globalization and open markets.[12] UN peace activity expanded in turn, from limited peacekeeping missions to incorporate new and more proactive elements of peace-making and peacebuilding which later developed into more robust peace enforcement capabilities.[13]

In short, in both the termination of the proxy wars and the rise of more forceful peace interventions, we witness the new peace activism of the UN.[14] But in addition to the UN, many other supranational

---

[10]Goldstein, "Winning the War on War", Chapter 2.
[11]Wallerstein and Sollenberg, "After the Cold War".
[12]Sawyer, "Violent Conflicts and Governance Challenges"; Young, "African Conflict Zone"; Pugh, Cooper, and Goodhand, *War Economies*.
[13]Tardy, "Critique of Robust Peacebuilding".
[14]Stedman, "New Interventionists".

organizations – the EU, NATO, OECD, World Bank, IMF, and AU – incorporated the goals of peacebuilding into their agendas. This expanding peace
activity inspired a surge in bi-lateral donor support for such activity (from
actors such as USAID, DfID, GIZ, and FMO),[15] and increasing funding
spurred a surge in the number of peace-related CSOs and non-governmental
organizations (NGOs), operating both at the international and national
levels.[16] Over time these non-governmental actors have become central to
peace interventions in conflict-affected and post-conflict societies and today
they function as implementation partners for global institutions which form
policy and set the agenda.

This expansion of activities led, inexorably, to an increasing number of
people hoping to work on peace processes and to the establishment of ever
more university and professional development programmes designed to
prepare students to pursue careers in peace intervention. Unsurprisingly,
this expansion in programmes and professional training has also led to the
professionalization of international peace intervention as a field of practice,[17]
and its domination by bureaucratic organizations which develop 'best practices' and 'tool-kits' for use in post-conflict states.[18] As critics have argued,
peace has largely come to be seen as something that can be built and maintained via the 'technocratic ministrations' of cadres of professionalized
practitioners.[19]

As such, the 'telos' of peacebuilding – the ideal peaceful society – is
rarely debated or considered.[20] It is assumed to replicate the 'Wilsonian'
liberal peace,[21] embodied in institutions of democracy, free-markets, and
the rule of law,[22] which the dominant quantitative literature claims to
have proven are key for long-term sustainable peace,[23] and which has
thus had significant influence on policy and funding decisions regarding
peace interventions. But, as recent literature has made clear, it is highly
problematic to assume linear relationships between establishing institutions
(electoral commissions, open markets, or courts) and local *experiences* of
those institutions.[24] Critics of the liberal peace, therefore, recognize these

---

[15]Paris, "Peacebuilding and the Limits"; De Soto and del Castillo, "Obstacles to Peacebuilding"; Richmond, Björkdahl, and Kapler, "Emerging EU Peacebuilding"; Williams, "Peace and Security Council"; Gheci, "Divided Partners".
[16]Van Tongeren et al., *People Building Peace II*; Pouligny, "Civil Society and Post-conflict"; Van Leeuwen, *Partners in Peace*; Edwards, Hulme, and Wallace, "NGOs in a Global Future"; Adejumobi, "Conflict and Peacebuilding"; Cubitt, *Local and Global Dynamics*; Paffenholz and Spurk, "Civil Society, Civil Engagement".
[17]Sending, *Why Peacebuilders Fail*, 3.
[18]Shaw, "Rethinking Truth and Reconciliation"; Donais, "Empowerment or Imposition", 23.
[19]Mac Ginty, "Hybrid Peace", 408.
[20]Denskus, "Challenging the International", 151.
[21]Paris, *At War's End*, 6.
[22]Doyle, "Three Pillars"; Paris, "Saving Liberal Peacebuilding".
[23]O'Neal et al., "The Liberal Peace"; Souva and Prins, "Liberal Peace Revisited".
[24]Millar, "Disaggregated Hybridity".

institutions as important less for peace than for the 'peace industry',[25] and as driven more by the concerns of technocrats than by those living in post-conflict societies.[26]

Recent publications regarding both hybridity and friction have illustrated how experiences of such interventions are more nuanced and unpredictable than once thought.[27] They recognize that interventions introduce new structures and norms into already complicated social, cultural, political, and economic environments and that the resulting 'hybrid peace' outcomes involve the 'mixing and melding of institutions, practices, rituals, and concepts generated through the interaction of coexisting, competing or complementary structures and norms'.[28] As a result, such outcomes are inherently unpredictable and emergent, and may aggravate old or even generate new conflict dynamics instead of promoting peace.[29]

Unfortunately however, while increasing demand has spurred the development of new methods to assess the impacts of peace interventions,[30] those methods have been dominated by standardized processes based on 'tick-box' evaluations counting *outputs* as opposed to *outcomes* and national-level variables used as proxies for more subtle impacts.[31] At the individual and community level, for example, we see the assessment of subtle phenomena such as 'engagement' via crude metrics such as attendance figures, and at a national level we see complex concepts such as 'justice' measured by the number of 'trial years' administered by a tribunal.[32] Even though the limitations of such quantification have been clearly articulated,[33] evaluation via such limited metrics is one of the primary skills required for young peace professionals and are seen as marketable skills that can be applied in diverse settings. The standardization of peace interventions, therefore, is mirrored in that of evaluation skills among both practitioners and academics, which only reproduces inadequate policy formation.[34]

---

[25] Mac Ginty, "Routine Peace", 289; Denskus, "Challenging the International", 151.

[26] Autesserre, *Trouble with the Congo*, 25–6.

[27] Mac Ginty, "Hybrid Peace"; Jarstad and Belloni, "Hybrid Peace Governance"; Millar, "Disaggregated Hybridity"; Björkdahl and Höglund, "Precarious Peacebuilding"; Millar, van der Lijn, and Verkoren, "Peacebuilding Plans"; Millar, "Expectations and Experiences".

[28] Millar, "Disaggregated Hybridity", 503.

[29] Millar, "Performative Memory".

[30] Paffenholz and Spurk, "Civil Society, Civil Engagement"; Blum, "Improving Peacebuilding Evaluation"; Duggan, "Transitional Justice on Trial"; Paffenholz, Abu-Nimer, and McCandless, "Peacebuilding and Development"; Bush and Duggan, "Evaluation in in Conflict Zones".

[31] Mac Ginty and Richmond, "Local Turn", 778.

[32] Sikkink and Booth Walling, "Impact of Human Rights"; Olsen, Payne, and Reiter, *Transitional Justice in Balance*.

[33] Jerven, *Poor Numbers*; Engle Merry and Wood, "Quantification and the Paradox".

[34] Müller and Bashar, "UNAMID".

Defining EPR

Leading PS scholars have recently noted an 'ethnographic turn' within the field.[35] Problematically, however, this includes many studies in which the term 'ethnographic' is applied to studies more appropriately labelled as 'qualitative'. The questions to ask are, therefore: How should PS distinguish between ethnographic and qualitative research? And what is the added value of such an approach? I argue that the term 'ethnography', following Ingold's characterization, should only be applied to research which includes 'long-term and open ended commitment, generous attentiveness, relational depth, and sensitivity to context'.[36] Research deploying the label without the substance implies the use of specific methods and the attainment of a particular form of knowledge distinct from what has been achieved. Alternatively, peace research which includes these characteristics may rightfully be described as Ethnographic as opposed to Qualitative and can provide substantively different forms of information regarding local experiences of peace intervention. But these distinctive characteristics are related to the time committed to, and subsequently the nature of, fieldwork.

Unlike Sociology, which incorporates some ethnographic research regarding domestic norms and institutions, Anthropology is the field most associated with international 'fieldwork'. 'Ethnographic fieldwork' is regularly recognized as one of the hallmarks of the discipline,[37] and it is via extended fieldwork that the researcher conducts participant observation; often considered the central practice of the discipline.[38] It is participant observation which embodies ethnography's generative tension by requiring the researcher to be at once the subjective participant and the objective observer, to 'step in and out' of another's perspective.[39] It is via such 'practical, personal and participatory experience in the field' that the Anthropologist comes to form knowledge.[40] But participant observation is not the only way Anthropologists collect data. Other classic methods include informal interviews, community mapping, and household censuses, for example. But, all of these processes share the aim of developing a contextualized interpretation – a 'translation from one cultural idiom or language to another'[41] – and this is a process which has always been understood to require extended periods of fieldwork.

Anthropology has developed its approach to this 'translation' substantially and recent scholarship has presented more nuanced interpretations of what counts as a 'field' and as 'ethnography', with contemporary scholars

---

[35]Mac Ginty and Richmond, "The Fallacy".
[36]Ibid.
[37]Bubandt and Otto, "Predicaments of Holism", 1.
[38]Robben and Sluka, "Fieldwork in Cultural Anthropology", 2.
[39]Powdermaker cited in Robben and Sluka, "Fieldwork in Cultural Anthopology", 13.
[40]Jackson, "Paths toward a Clearing", 3.
[41]Marcus, "Ethnography in/of the World", 100.

addressing multi-sited or mobile fields and reframing ethnography as the study of chains, flows, circulations, frictions, and culture as process.[42] In such contemporary conceptions, however, long-term engagement with the fields or processes under study – even when multi-sited, mobile, and flexible – remains central.[43] Similarly, the 'Writing Culture' debate of the 70s and 80s led to further changes and a new emphasis on reflexivity;[44] the 'need to be critically conscious of what one is doing as one does it';[45] an idea often echoed.[46] Such research recognizes that the reality to be interpreted and presented in the text is constructed collaboratively with research subjects and over time. Critical self-reflection is therefore required for ethnographic research. A reflection that itself demands long-term engagement with subjects in the field.

But to what extent should EPR mirror the contemporary approach to ethnography as conducted in Anthropology? There are many fruitful Anthropological works exploring the dynamics of war and peace,[47] and others which examine local or community experiences of conflict, transition, and peace.[48] It is partially the impact of such work that has inspired the use of ethnographic methodologies as alternative means for evaluating peace interventions within PS.[49] However, while much can be learned from these studies – and the difference between these influential Anthropological studies and ethnographically inspired work within PS is one of degree and not of kind – the different assumptions and expectations of the two fields do demand recognition of important differences between ethnography within contemporary Anthropology and the deployment of ethnographic methods as a means to provide *contextualized evaluations* within PS.

For example, the subject matter of Anthropology is qualitatively different to that in Peace Research. Anthropology is, in its broadest sense, 'a sustained and disciplined inquiry into the conditions and potentials of human life'.[50] Anthropological studies primarily examine a group, a sub-group, a dynamic, or a particular phenomenon, all of which will build to this broader understanding of human life. In addition, as a result of its association with colonialism,[51] and its instrumentalization during wartime,[52]

---

[42]Appadurai, *Modernity at Large*; Tsing, *Friction*; Mosse, "Anthropology of International Development"; Carse, "2013 in Sociocultural Anthropology"; see also contributions to Millar, Ethnographic Peace Research.
[43]Gupta and Ferguson, "Beyond Culture"; Hannerz, "Being There"; Marcus, "Ethnography in/of the World".
[44]Clifford and Marcus, "Writing Culture"; Davies, *Reflexive Ethnography*, 10.
[45]Crapanzano, "Heart of the Discipline", 56.
[46]Diphoorn, "Emotionality of Participation"; Davies and Spencer, *Emotions in the Field*.
[47]Richards, *Fighting*; Vigh, *Navigating Terrains*; Coulter, *Bush Wives*; Lombard, *State of Rebellion*.
[48]Shaw, "Memory Frictions"; Theidon, *Intimate Enemies*; Park, *Reappeared*; Bräuchler, *Cultural Dimensions*; Honwana, *Child Soldiers*. Nordstrom, *Shadows of War*; Nordstrom and Robben, *Fieldwork under Fire*; Das, *Life and Words*; Hinton and Hinton, *Genocide and Mass Violence*.
[49]Denskus, "Challenging the International"; Denskus, "Peacebuilding Does Not"; Millar, *Ethnographic Approach*.
[50]Ingold, *Being Alive*, 3.
[51]Lewis, "Anthropology and Colonialism"; Pels, "What has Anthropology Learned".
[52]Chambers, "Applied Anthropology"; Robben "Anthropology and the Iraq War".

Anthropology has developed a deep ambivalence towards policy and practice. PS, on the other hand, is both more focused and more applied. It is the study of the multi-disciplinary dynamics undergirding two very specific phenomena – conflict and peace – and is an avowedly normative field, with the explicit purpose of impacting policy and practice. It seeks to gain knowledge for use, to 'transfer' that knowledge to policy-makers and practitioners, and to influence conflict resolution and peacebuilding.[53]

Quite distinct from Anthropology, therefore, the benefits of long-term fieldwork for PS are partially instrumental in nature and what I propose here is a pragmatic approach to deploying ethnographic methods for assessment purposes. It is exactly such a positivist or instrumental approach that Ingold is responding to when he argues against the application of the 'ethnographic' label to methods more appropriately described as qualitative. He questions whether ethnography can or should be deployed instrumentally, or if ethnography innately requires an epistemology that negates a positivist or instrumentalist stance.[54] While I sympathize with these concerns, this paper does not engage in this debate, instead proposing that PS can learn from the substantial insight provided by Anthropological studies, including those of conflict and peace, and incorporate these lessons into the potentially controversial use of ethnography as a pragmatic means of assessment.

This is necessary because policy-makers have not been as receptive to Anthropological findings from conflict-affected or post-conflict settings as they have been to the claims of other disciplines (such as Economics, Political Science, and Law). Peace scholars, therefore, must incorporate research methodologies that allow more sensitivity to issues of diversity and culture, while still retaining the ability to speak to, and (importantly) to be heard by, policy-makers and practitioners. EPR seeks to do this by conducting studies that *aspire* to the qualities Ingold described but which are not ethnography in the Anthropological tradition.[55] It is my argument that while this research differs from Anthropological ethnography, it still requires extended periods of fieldwork, and it is for this reason that the benefits of such fieldwork must be clearly described and evidenced.

Key benefits of long-term fieldwork: time, chance, and change

The goal of this section is to evidence the added value that is gained from living within and witnessing the many challenges of a post-conflict setting. As will be illustrated, an understanding of everyday life in post-conflict contexts cannot be gleaned from interviews, focus groups, or observations alone (even when conducted among non-elite locals). Indeed, it is the broader

---

[53]Boulding, "Future Direction", 343–4.
[54]Ingold, *Being Alive.*
[55]Ingold, "That's Enough about Ethnography", 384.

context of people's lives that shapes their ideas and opinions, their expectations and experiences.[56] As such, only familiarity with that context allows the researcher to interpret how people understand and represent their world. In what follows, I describe three benefits of long-term fieldwork: time, chance, and change. I will illustrate why each is so important to an EPR approach with examples of the added value of such research from my past work in rural Sierra Leone.

This research spanned a total of 19 months in-country. This includes 2 months in 2007 and 10 months in 2008/2009 during which I conducted an evaluation of the local experiences of the Truth and Reconciliation Commission (TRC) in and around the city of Makeni in Northern Sierra Leone, as well as 6 months in 2012 and 1 month in 2013 during which I evaluated the impacts of a large Bio-energy project in 12 villages within the project's 40,000 hectare land-lease area. Both of these studies involved long-term engagement with these communities, participant observation, and semi-structured interviews designed to assess understandings and experiences of the interventions. I have since published more than a dozen peer-reviewed articles presenting these data, as well as a couple of papers describing the benefits of such ethnographic assessments as a means to understand how and why interventions are experienced as they are in local settings. However, I have never before written specifically of the substantial added value of long-term fieldwork above and beyond what could be gathered by the same methods (interviews, observations, site visits), if they had been carried out over weeks instead of months. This will be my task here.

Time

Obviously more time on the ground produces more formal 'data' (more interviews, more observations, additional site visits, etc.), and in this sense its value would be clear to most researchers, even those not conducting ethnographic studies but who want to collect more surveys, include more cases, or extend a longitudinal study. But while additional data are *valuable* for almost all research, in ethnography time in the field is *required* for accurate interpretation of that data. Most of my formal 'data' during my first period of research regarding the TRC (between 2007 and 2009), for example, was collected over a 10-month period. This included more than 60 semi-structured interviews and participant observation with people living both in the Northern town of Makeni and in a small village outside Makeni. While it would have been perfectly possible to collect exactly that number of interviews and visit those 2 sites in a matter of weeks instead of 10 months, a clear and accurate understanding of that data required an extended period of fieldwork.

---

[56]Mac Ginty, "Peacekeeping and Data", 701.

Additional time in country, for example, allowed me to more fully and intimately engage with the two communities. It allowed me to develop relationships with individuals and families, to participate in community events, and simply to engage in informal conversations about everyday life. Such informal conversations occurred on friend's front porches or on walks through town, at the small college campus in Makeni or while watching sporting events, and the topics could roam from the weather to witches, from football to religion, and from politics to culture. Such informal interactions provide a contextual perspective that multiplies manyfold the substantive understanding of the formal 'data'. It allows the researcher to understand the context from within which actors understand their own lifeworld and view the interventions of external agencies. This is the added value of long-term fieldwork, which would be clear to Ethnographers working within Anthropology, but is often overlooked or considered only tangentially by Peace Researchers who rarely spend extended time with the 'beneficiaries' of peace interventions.

For example, it was only by getting to know, working alongside, and speaking regularly with locals of different faiths that I could fully grasp the importance of religion and the belief in unseen powers in rural Sierra Leone. Intellectually it is easy to conceive of individuals believing in the everyday presence and agency of spirits, devils, and their own ancestors; and Anthropological literature regarding Sierra Leone can impress this upon the reader.[57] But coming to a full appreciation of the deeper force and implications of this took time in the setting, speaking to people about the power of society magic, seeing the deep fear of being witched, and discussing also my own faith. Such experiences struck home the reality of these forces for Sierra Leoneans; forces which, as I have described elsewhere in more ethnographic fashion, impacted on local experiences of the TRC.[58] Without extended time in this setting, engaging with local people, this more grounded interpretation of my formal data would never have been possible.

However, there are also other benefits to long-term fieldwork. Additional time allowed me to conduct a very useful second translation of all of my interviews, for example, during which I sat side-by-side with a second translator and asked questions when his interpretations of interviewee's words differed from the original translation. This process took an inordinate amount of time, but it also provided insight into the meaning of the language used by local people which, first, would not be obvious to a non-native, and second, was not obvious from the initial translation. As a result, quite a lot of important data from the interviews themselves was only recognized due to the extended time I spent participating in this second translation process and developing additional contextual understanding. Indeed, the time spent on this process

---

[57]Bledsoe and Robey, "Arabic Literacy and Secrecy"; Murphy, "Sublime Dance"; Shaw, "Memory Frictions".
[58]Millar, "Between Western Theory"; Milllar, "Lef Ma Case".

proved just as important as that spent on collecting the interviews in the first place.

In addition, having this time on the ground, and my developing awareness of the culturally situated concerns and expectations of local actors, allowed the evolution of my research methodology from a flawed initial approach to one which would eventually produce quite unique findings. Following earlier research indicating that ritual and symbolism were important elements of healing and reconciliation in Truth Commissions,[59] I had originally planned to examine this aspect of the TRC's work in Makeni. However, after four months in the country it became clear that this approach was not really applicable as almost nobody in Makeni remembered or cared about symbolic, ritual, or ceremonial aspects of the TRC's public hearing process. Quite to the contrary, people in Makeni, as I have written elsewhere, were more interested in employment, educational opportunities, restarting farms, and rebuilding homes than they were with symbolism or even forgiveness.[60] While the literature at the time argued that ritual would be central to success, spending time with local individuals and in local communities made it clear that priorities lay elsewhere.

Without long-term fieldwork this might have been disastrous. However, as it was this realization – after about four months in the field, did not prove fatal to my research because over those first months I was also coming to understand what was important to people in Makeni. As a result, I was able to reconsider the topics I wanted to explore in my research and identify a more important research question. This was only possible, however, because I had time; because I both had the initial four months of interaction and observation to realize what other questions might be pertinent to local people, and, of course, because I still had six months left to answer them.

Chance

The second key benefit of conducting long-term fieldwork is chance, or the unanticipated communications, interactions, and events that occur when you are somewhere for an extended period and must, therefore, live your life as opposed to only conducting research. As others have noted,[61] during long-term fieldwork chance encounters, weird miscommunications, and ser-endipitous calamities provide just as much insight about a setting as the formal research itself, and, more importantly, they provide substantive knowledge of the context within which formal data are nested. I will illustrate this through the quite simple example of institutional decay.

---

[59]Bozzoli, "Public Ritual"; Kelsall, "Truth, Lies, Ritual".
[60]Millar, "Evaluations of Truth"; Millar, "Evaluations of Justice"; Millar, "Local Experiences".
[61]Okely, *Anthropological Practice*; Crapanzano, "At the Heart", 60.

On the face of it, this problem is easily measured and quantified. Scholars and governments regularly claim to assess the quality of institutions via national-level metrics. We can think here of infant mortality rates as a measure of healthcare, graduation rates for education, crime rates for security, or gross domestic product for economic development. However, long-term fieldwork provides the researcher a greater understanding of the lived reality – or unreality – of such national figures. Take, for example, the healthcare system. Until 2013, the Sierra Leonean healthcare system was regularly lauded as a success of the post-conflict period for its provision of free healthcare to women, infants, and children,[62] and an increase in life expectancy by 5 years between 2000 and 2008.[63] However, as the Ebola epidemic made clear, and as anyone who had spent substantial time there well knew, healthcare in Sierra Leone was neither successfully rebuilt nor sufficiently resourced. Much like the bloating of the national registers due to non-existent ghost nurses,[64] the improvements in healthcare and the affordability and accessibility of the system were largely figments of political imagination. Anyone visiting a hospital or clinic in rural Sierra Leone for actual treatment in the past decade knew this.

And this is where chance comes in. If a researcher spends three weeks in-country, staying at nice clean hotels, eating at air-conditioned restaurants, and being driven around in a large SUV, they may never actually have to visit a hospital, a pharmacy, or a clinic except on a guided tour by exactly those actors who are selling the image of a functional system. Over three or four carefully sanitized weeks they may never get malaria or typhoid, pick up a Tumbu fly infection, or get into an accident. But when you live without power or air conditioning, drink the water, get bitten by the mosquitos, and travel around by Okada (motorcycle taxi), you will eventually have all of these experiences. It is only then that you might see the healthcare system in action; or perhaps inaction.

I have had many such experiences during my periods of fieldwork. I have required treatment for malaria three times, typhoid once, and both I and a number of friends and acquaintances have experienced various injuries requiring medical assistance. While none of these experiences were pleasurable of course, and I am not trying to romanticize the dangers of fieldwork or promote unsafe practice to young colleagues, I also know that these experiences provided invaluable insight into how local people experience healthcare institutions in the country. If I had reviewed national healthcare statistics and been shown around a hospital by its director, a doctor, or a politician, I would have been shown the cleanest wards, the most capable nurses, and the

[62]Donnelly, "How did Sierra Leone".
[63]WHO, World Health Statistics 2010.
[64]Witter, Wurie, and Bertone, "Free Health Care Initiative", 9.

brightest theatres. It was only by experiencing the system first hand – visiting my research assistant's mother after her heart attack or a friend who had had a motorcycle accident (and later died) – that I came close to seeing it through the eyes of the patients. In other words, it was only because I was there long enough to need to interact with the health system that I had those experiences.

The same applies to the security institutions. The police, for example, have seen an enormous amount of reform and investment over the past 15 years.[65] Millions have been spent retraining police leadership and officers throughout the country, reequipping the force with vehicles and weapons, and rewriting rules and regulations. While few consider these efforts fully successful, studies have been somewhat optimistic about the process, recognizing the substantial challenges of complete reform.[66] However, much like the health-sector, having engaged with the police services on various occasions, I completely understand why the formal legal institutions are the second best option for the average Sierra Leonean, who is still much more likely to rely on the chiefly courts or the traditional diviners.[67]

Shortly after my 2012 fieldwork, for example, my research assistant was arrested and held by the police in a town on the highway to Freetown, who then demanded the equivalent of £100 for his release. I was informed that this was because he was known to work for me, a white European, and so he should have access to the money. He was held for weeks in a concrete prison cell filled with other offenders, sleeping on the floor, and relying on friends and family from Makeni for food each day. He was told that if he did not produce the money he would be sent directly to Pademba Road prison, the central prison in Freetown at which the most dangerous and violent prisoners are incarcerated. This is not particularly remarkable in the Sierra Leone penal system where, indeed, there is a long history of detention without trial.[68]

It is because of such experiences that few locals in rural Sierra Leone choose to engage the police. Just as with teachers, nurses, and other civil servants, police often go long periods without their salaries and, partially as a result of this, often take advantage of their position of authority to acquire much needed resources. Instead, local communities in rural Sierra Leone primarily rely on diviners to identify criminals and on Chiefly Courts to adjudicate conflicts. These examples regarding both the healthcare system and the police forces in rural Sierra Leone illustrate the value of the communications, interactions, and events that occur during research not due to meticulous planning, but due to chance. However, such experiences will not occur to researchers visiting a setting for only a few weeks. Chance itself requires time.

---

[65]Gbla, "Security Sector Reform"; Krogstad, "Security, Development, and Force".
[66]Horn, Olonisakin, and Peake, "United Kingdom-led Security".
[67]Sawyer, "Remove or Reform".
[68]US State Department, "Sierra Leone 2015"; Kamara, "Discharged Inmates".

Change

This brings us to the final key benefit of long-term fieldwork; the opportunity to experience, observe, and investigate change. It is clear of course that change can best be observed through time and the less time one spends examining any given phenomena the less change can be observed. This is why longitudinal studies are appropriate for examining change in quantitative research, but the same principle applies in ethnographic studies.[69] During my own periods of extended fieldwork this has been most apparent in the differences within Makeni between research conducted in 2008/2009 and that carried out four years later, in 2012/2013.

The first example of this change is the incredible increase in food, housing, and land prices between these two periods. This rise in costs is related to two primary dynamics, one global and one more local. Globally the credit crunch after 2008/2009 and new bio-energy projects throughout the world led to an increase in the global prices for both fuel and food,[70] which led to substantial rises in the cost of living throughout Sierra Leone. More locally, the influx of workers from other areas of Sierra Leone into Makeni as a result of the bio-energy project I was studying in 2012/2013, put additional pressure on the labour, housing, and food markets. This occurred both because expatriate employees and educated Sierra Leonean workers relocating to Makeni drove up the price of housing within the town itself, and because the substantial influx of less educated labourers from other regions of the country into the villages within the land-lease area of the project (located some miles West of Makeni) drove up the prices of both food and housing for people in the villages.

These changes were substantial and particularly important because interventions that may have been assessed positively in 2008/2009 because they could provide minimal material or economic benefits were less likely to be experienced positively in 2012/2013 when the value of those benefits had depreciated. As I have reported elsewhere,[71] in 2012 labourers working for the bio-energy company were making approximately $75 per month. This was commensurate with the salaries of local NGO workers I volunteered with in 2008 and at that time would have been substantial money for village residents. However, by 2012 this income was less than half of what villagers estimated they would need to support a family. Women in the villages in 2012, for example, described being unable to save as they once had for their children's school fees because all of their money was spent on food, while many people complained of eating only one meal per day. Perhaps most difficult were the experiences of those local youth from the villages who had been

---

[69]Rosaldo, "Grief"; Diphoorn, "Emotionality of Participation", 208–9.
[70]Zoomers, "Globalisation and the Foreignisation".
[71]Millar, "Investing in Peace"; Millar, "Coopting Authority".

unable to gain permanent employment with the company; squeezed out by the more educated and urban new arrivals, they found themselves now both landless and without a salary to compensate.

The second change I observed over this time would almost certainly only be noted by a researcher spending enough time in country to interact with local youth, and particularly young men in Makeni. This was a distinct increase in aggressive responses to or expressions of hostility towards expatriates. Indeed, during my first period of extended fieldwork in 2008/2009 I never had one such experience in Makeni, nor did anyone I spoke with show animosity towards or fear of expatriates. Indeed, local people regularly expressed their thanks to the UK and other actors for their role in ending the conflict and praised the work of the few expatriates who were in Makeni at the time (usually less than 20 throughout my 2008/2009 fieldwork).

However, by the time of my 2012 fieldwork this had changed substantially. The numbers of expatriates had multiplied 10-fold, to more than 200, and the kind of work they were doing had also changed significantly. Whereas four years earlier the primary fields of intervention were healthcare (doctors and nurses) and development (NGO volunteers), by 2012 the average expatriate was working for the bio-energy company, one of the nearby mining companies, or the companies building infrastructure for these industries. From the initial groups of nurses, doctors, and volunteers in 2008/2009, Makeni was now hosting industrial farmers, engineers, and miners. The social environments in which these expatriates interacted with locals had changed accordingly, from local bars in which the handful of expatriates were a small minority, to expatriate hang-outs where most locals in attendance were either working behind the bar, serving food, or, in the worst cases, providing 'comfort' for the now male-dominated clientele.

Not surprisingly the response from young Sierra Leonean men to this new dynamic was negative and during my second period of extended fieldwork in 2012 there were regular expressions of hostility towards expatriates. Some Okada drivers would refuse to pick up white passengers at all, while I often received hostile stares in the streets. One evening, food was thrown in my face as I passed a group of young men on an Okada. This new dynamic mirrored the bunker mentality among many of the expatriates working for the companies who were working in the region.[72] Unlike the expatriates in 2008/2009, who engaged with local communities to shop for food or have a drink, by 2012 there was no reason to enter the local market, drink at a local bar or eat at a local restaurant as two supermarkets and various bars had appeared to cater almost exclusively to expatriates. Positive interaction between the two communities was, as a result, quite rare.

---

[72]Millar, "Coopting Authority".

But, again, this change would be invisible to a researcher who had not been engaged over this relatively long period. A researcher staying in Makeni for a month in 2008 or in 2012 might not have interacted enough with local people to assess their feelings towards expatriates. If they had reached such an assessment in one of these periods, it would either be that people in Makeni are quite friendly to expats or that people in Makeni (and particularly young men) are quite hostile towards expats. But it is more likely that no change would have been noted as the hostile acts themselves are occurrences of chance that simply may not have happened during a quick site visit or if travelling by SUV instead of Okada and staying in hotels instead of local housing. In this way, this example makes clear the relationship between time, chance, and change.

As I have discussed elsewhere,[73] this hostility is concerning both because it highlights the very real frustrations towards international interventions among local young men, and because it is a sign of the failure of the peace-building process to provide the economic opportunities required in a state where the conflict itself was rooted in economic inequalities.[74] As such, interpreting the nature and drivers of this dynamic – and others like it – are key to assessing post-conflict intervention and providing nuanced suggestions for post-conflict policy formation in this and other cases. But such assessment requires not bounded research questions, short-term field-visits, and reliance on a limited sample of respondents. It requires long-term fieldwork and the substantively different forms of information such research provides.

Conclusion

This article presents a relatively simple argument. As support and funding for international peace interventions grew in the post-Cold War period, so the standardization of what came to be labelled the 'peace industry' developed apace, producing cadres of peacebuilding professionals armed with best practices and technocratic skills. At the same time, and in response to the increased funding for and prominence of peace intervention, funders demanded more assessment of peace interventions and so M&E skills also came to be a sought after within the peace industry. However, these skills too have become technocratic and standardized, producing tick-box assessment mechanisms collecting quantitative data on *outputs* and rarely more substantive evaluations of local experiences. Such approaches to M&E are today accepted as best-practice among peacebuilding organizations, much as quantitative large-N studies of state-level data came much earlier to dominate Peace Research and have the most influence on policy.

---

[73]Millar, "Local Experiences".
[74]Peters and Richards, "Why We Fight"; Humphreys and Weinstein, "Who Fights?", 439.

However, a great amount of recent literature argues against a simplified and linear interpretation that links new or reformed institutions inherently with a more sustainable peace. The local turn literature in critical peacebuilding, with its emphases on the everyday, hybridity, and resistance, describes a much more agonistic process by which post-conflict peace is constructed,[75] and the turn to non-linearity, friction, and complexity emphasizes the unpredictable nature of peace intervention effects. This has paralleled an ethnographic turn within IR which this paper certainly contributes to.[76] However, what I hope to discourage is the easy appropriation of the ethnographic label for research which is more appropriately called qualitative. That is, for research which collects qualitative data in the post-conflict setting, but without *aspiring* to 'long-term and open ended commitment, generous attentiveness, relational depth, and sensitivity to context'.[77]

The key purpose of this paper, therefore, has been to articulate how ethnography differs from qualitative work and to illustrate the significant added value of long-term fieldwork for an EPR approach. I emphasized three key added benefits of long-term fieldwork – *time, chance,* and *change* – and argued that each provides the researcher additional understanding of the sociocultural context within which data must be understood. Long-term fieldwork may not be necessary to collect qualitative data, but the substantive understanding of what that data mean – particularly when collected in sociocultural settings foreign to the researcher – requires the researcher to conduct extended fieldwork within the context of the study. In my own case the added time such fieldwork provided for getting to know the context and the people, for conducting a secondary transcription and analysis of my data, for the evolution of my research question and approach, for the chance encounters, weird miscommunications, and serendipitous calamities that gave unexpected insights to how Sierra Leonean society functions, and for the recognition, observation, and analysis of change, were invaluable and greatly enhanced the substance of my findings.

I do not claim that all research must incorporate long-term fieldwork, nor argue that the approach to EPR I am proposing must be the only or the final approach. Some anthropologists would surely suggest that my approach does not go far enough, that the instrumental or positivist approach I have taken harkens back to an era of positivist Anthropology long since rejected in that discipline. Others may argue that long-term fieldwork is helpful, but not required, that short periods of fieldwork with more focused research questions can be even more valuable. My intention here is to spur exactly those methodological debates which must be had in response to the ongoing

---

[75]Richmond, "Resistance and the Post-Liberal", 676.
[76]Vrasti, "Strange Case of Ethnography".
[77]Ingold, "That's Enough about Ethnography", 384.

'ethnographic turn' within IR and PS. All I sought to do here is respond to the increasing tendency to present qualitative research as ethnographic research without a real engagement with what the term means. By focusing on the added benefits of long-term fieldwork – of time, chance, and change – for understanding post-conflict dynamics, I hope that this article can be taken not as disparaging purely qualitative work, but as highlighting the distinction between the two.

Disclosure statement

No potential conflict of interest was reported by the author.

Funding

This work was supported by Carnegie Trust for the Universities of Scotland and Radboud Universiteit Nijmegen.

Bibliography

Adejumobi, Said. "Conflict and Peacebuilding in West Africa: The Role of Civil Society and the African Union." *Conflict, Security & Development* 4, no. 1 (2004): 59–77.

Appadurai, Arjun. *Modernity at Large: Cultural Dimensions of Globalization.* Minneapolis: University of Minnesota Press, 1996.

Autesserre, Severine. *The Trouble with the Congo: Local Violence and the Failure of International Peacebuilding.* New York: Cambridge University Press, 2010.

Björkdahl, Annika, and Kristine Höglund. "Precarious Peacebuilding: Friction in Global-Local Encounters." *Peacebuilding* 1, no. 3 (2013): 289–99.

Bledsoe, Caroline H. and Kenneth M. Robey. "Arabic Literacy and Secrecy among the Mende of Sierra Leone." *Man: New Series* 21, no. 2 (1986): 202–26.

Blum, Andrew. "Improving Peacebuilding Evaluation: A Whole-of-Field Approach." United States Institute of Peace, Special Report #280, June 2011. www.usip.org/sites/default/files/SR-Improving-Peace-Building-Evaluation.pdf (accessed October 13, 2016).

Boulding, Kenneth. "Future Directions in Conflict and Peace Studies." *Journal of Conflict Resolution* 22, no. 2 (1978): 342–54.

Bozzoli, Belinda. "Public Ritual and Private Transition: The Truth Commission in Alexandra Township, South Africa 1996." *African Studies* 57, no. 2 (1998): 167–95.

Bräuchler, Birgit. *The Cultural Dimensions of Peace: Decentralization and Reconciliation in Indonesia*. Basingstoke: Palgrave MacMillan, 2015.

Bubandt, Nils and Ton Otto. "Anthropology and the Predicaments of Holism," in *Experiments in Holism: Theory and Practice in Contemporary Anthropology*, ed. Nils Bubandt and Ton Otto, 1–15. Malden: Wiley-Blackwell, 2010.

Bush, Kenneth, and Colleen Duggan. "Evaluation in Conflict Zones: Methodological and Ethical Challenges." *Journal of Peacebuilding and Development* 8, no. 2 (2013): 5–25.

Carse, Ashley. "The Year 2013 in Sociocultural Anthropology: Cultures of Circulation and Anthropological Facts." *American Anthropologist* 116, no. 2 (2014): 390–403.

Catholic Relief Services. *GAIN Peacebuilding Indicators*. Baltimore, MD: PQSD Publications Team, 2010. www.learningforpeace.unicef.org/wp-content/uploads/2014/02/CRS-GAIN-Peace-Indicator-Manual.pdf (accessed October 13, 2016).

Chambers, Erve. "Applied Anthropology in the Post-Vietnam Era: Anticipations and Ironies." *Annual Review of Anthropology* 16 (1987): 309–37.

Chandler, David. "Peacebuilding and the Politics of Non-linearity: Rethinking 'Hidden' Agency and 'Resistance'." *Peacebuilding* 1, no. 1 (2013): 17–32.

Clifford, James and George E. Marcus. *Writing Culture: The Poetics and Politics of Ethnography*. Berkeley: University of California Press, 1986.

Coulter, Chris. *Bush Wives and Girl Soldiers: Women's Lives through War and Peace in Sierra Leone*. Ithaca, NY: Cornell University Press, 2009.

Crapanzano, Vincent. "'At the Heart of the Discipline': Critical Reflections on Fieldwork," in *Emotions in the Field: The Psychology and Anthropology of Fieldwork Experience*, eds. James Davies and Dimitrina Spencer, 55–78. Stanford, CA: Stanford University Press, 2010.

Cubitt, Christine. *Local and Global Dynamics of Peacebuilding: Post-Conflict Peacebuilding in Sierra Leone*. London: Routledge, 2012.

Das, Veena. *Life and Words: Violence and the Descent into the Ordinary*. Berkeley, CA: University of California Press, 2007.

Davies, Charlotte Aull. *Reflexive Ethnography: A Guide to Researching Selves and Others*. London: Routledge, 2008.

Davies, James and Dimitrina Spencer. *Emotions in the Field: The Psychology and Anthropology of Fieldwork Experience*. Stanford, CA: Stanford University Press, 2010.

Denskus, Tobias. "Peacebuilding Does Not Build Peace," in *Deconstructing Development Discourse: Buzzwords and Fuzzwords*, ed. Andrea Cornwall and Deborah Eade, 235–43. Oxford: Oxfam, 2010.

Denskus, Tobias. "Challenging the International Peacebuilding Evaluation Discourse with Qualitative Methodologies." *Evaluation and Program Planning* 35, no. 1 (2012): 148–53.

De Soto, Alvaro, and Graciana del Castillo. "Obstacles to Peacebuilding Revisited." *Global Governance* 22, no. 2 (2016): 209–27.

Diphoorn, Tessa. "The Emotionality of Participation: Various Modes of Participation in Ethnographic Fieldwork on Private Policing in Durban, South Africa." *Journal of Contemporary Anthropology* 42, no. 2 (2012): 201–25.

Donais, Timothy. "Empowerment or Imposition? Dilemmas of Local Ownership in Post-conflict Peacebuilding Processes." *Peace & Change* 34, no. 1 (2009): 3–26.

Donnelly, John. "How did Sierra Leone Provide Free Health Care?" *The Lancet* 377, no. 9775 (2011): 1393–96.

Doyle, Michael W. "Three Pillars of the Liberal Peace." *American Political Science Review* 99, no. 3 (2005): 463–66.

Duggan, Colleen. ed. "Transitional Justice on Trial: Evaluating its Impact." *International Journal of Transitional Justice* (Special Issue) 4, no. 3 (2010).

Edwards, Michael, David Hulme and Tine Wallace. "NGOs in a Global Future: Marrying Local Delivery to Worldwide Leverage." *Public Administration and Development* 19, no. 2 (1999): 117–36.

Engle Merry, Sally and Summer Wood. "Quantification and the Paradox of Measurement: Translating Children's Rights in Tanzania." *Current Anthropology* 56, no. 2 (2015): 205–29.

Gbla, Osman. "Security Sector Reform under International Tutelage in Sierra Leone." *International Peacekeeping* 13, no. 1 (2006): 78–93.

Gheciu, Alexandru. "Divided Partners: The Challenges of NATO-NGO Cooperation in Peacebuilding Operations." *Global Governance* 17, no. 1 (2011): 95–113.

Goldstein, Joshua S. *Winning the War on War: The Decline of Armed Conflict Worldwide*. London: Penguin Books, 2011.

Gupta, Akhil, and James Ferguson. "Beyond 'Culture': Space, Identity, and the Politics of Difference." *Cultural Anthropology* 7, no. 1 (1992): 6–23.

Hannerz, Ulf. "Being there ... and there ... and there! Reflections on Multi-Site Ethnography." *Ethnography* 4, no. 2 (2003): 201–16.

Hinton, Devon E. and Alexander L. Hinton. *Genocide and Mass Violence: Memory, Symptom, and Recovery*. New York: Cambridge University Press, 2015.

Honwana, Alcinda. *Child Soldiers in Africa*. Philadelphia: University of Pennsylvania Press, 2006.

Horn, Adrian, Funmi Olonisakin, and Gordon Peake. "United Kingdom-led Security Sector Reform in Sierra Leone." *Civil Wars* 8, no. 2 (2006): 109–23.

Humphreys, Macartan, and Jeremy M. Weinstein. "Who Fights? The Determinants of Participation in Civil War." *American Journal of Political Science* 52, no. 2 (2008): 436–55.

Ingold, Tim. *Being Alive: Essays on Movement, Knowledge and Description*. London: Routledge, 2010.

Ingold, Tim. "That's Enough about Ethnography!" *HAU: Journal of Ethnographic Theory* 4, no. 1 (2014): 383–95.

Jackson, Michael. *Paths toward a Clearing: Radical Empiricism and Ethnographic Enquiry*. Bloomington: Indiana University Press, 1989.

Jakobson, Peter Viggo. "The Transformation of United Nations Peace Operations in the 1990s: Adding Globalization to the Conventional 'End of the Cold War Explanation'." *Cooperation and Conflict* 37, no. 3 (2002): 267–82.

Jarstad, Anna K., and Roberto Belloni. eds. "Hybrid Peace Governance." *Global Governance* (Special Issue) 18, no. 1 (2012).

Jerven, Morten. *Poor Numbers: How we are Misled by African Development Statistics and What Do to About It*. Ithaca, NY: Cornell University Press, 2013.

Kamara, Patrick Jaiah. "Discharged Inmates Tell Painful Stories after 8 Years on Remand." *Concord Times*. June 22, 2016. www.slconcordtimes.com/discharged-inmates-tell-painful-stories-after-8-years-on-remand/ (accessed May 29, 2017).

Kelsall, Timothy. "Truth, Lies, Ritual: Preliminary Reflections on the Truth and Reconciliation Commission." *Human Rights Quarterly* 27, no. 2 (2005): 361–91.

Krogstad, Erlend Groner. "Security, Development, and Force: Revisiting Police Reform in Sierra Leone." *African Affairs* 111, no. 443 (2011): 261–80.

Lewis, Diane. "Anthropology and Colonialism." *Current Anthropology* 14, no. 5 (1973): 581–602.

Lombard, Luisa. *State of Rebellion: Violence and Intervention in the Central African Republic*. London: Zed Books, 2016.

Mac Ginty, Roger. "Hybrid Peace: The Interaction between Top-Down and Bottom-Up Peace." *Security Dialogue* 41, no. 4 (2010): 391–412.

Mac Ginty, Roger. "Routine Peace: Technocracy and Peacebuilding." *Cooperation and Conflict* 47, no. 3 (2012): 287–308.

Mac Ginty, Roger. "Peacekeeping and Data." *International Peacekeeping* 24, no. 5 (2017): 695–705.

Mac Ginty, Roger, and Oliver P. Richmond. "The Local Turn in Peacebuilding: A Critical Agenda for Peace." *Third World Quarterly* 34, no. 5 (2013): 763–83.

Mac Ginty, Roger, and Oliver P. Richmond. "The Fallacy of Constructing Hybrid Political Orders: A Reappraisal of the Hybrid Turn in Peacebuilding." *International Peacekeeping* 23, no. 2 (2016): 219–39.

Marcus, Clifford. "Ethnography in/of the World System: The Emergence of Multi-sited Ethnography." *Annual Review of Anthropology* 24 (1995): 95–117.

Millar, Gearoid. "Local Evaluations of Truth Telling in Sierra Leone: Getting at 'Why' Though a Qualitative Case Study Analysis." *International Journal of Transitional Justice* 4, no. 4 (2010): 477–96.

Millar, Gearoid. "Between Western Theory and Local Practice: Cultural Impediments to Truth-Telling Sierra Leone." *Conflict Resolution Quarterly* 29, no. 2 (2011): 177–99.

Millar, Gearoid. "Local Evaluations of Justice through Truth Telling in Sierra Leone: Postwar Needs and Transitional Justice." *Human Rights Quarterly* 12, no. 4 (2012): 515–35.

Millar, Gearoid. "'A lef ma Case fo God': Faith and Agency in Sierra Leone's Postwar Reconciliation." *Peace and Conflict: Journal of Peace Psychology* 18, no. 2 (2012): 131–43.

Millar, Gearoid. "Expectations and Experiences of Peacebuilding in Sierra Leone: Parallel Peacebuilding Processes and Compound Friction." *International Peacekeeping* 20, no. 2 (2013): 189–203.

Millar, Gearoid. *An Ethnographic Approach to Peacebuilding: Understanding Local Experiences in Transitional States*. London: Routledge, 2014.

Millar, Gearoid. "Disaggregated Hybridity: Why Hybrid Institutions Do Not Produce Predictable Experiences of Peace." *Journal of Peace Research* 51, no. 4 (2014): 501–14.

Millar, Gearoid. "Performative Memory and Re-victimization: Truth-telling and Provocation in Sierra Leone." *Memory Studies* 8, no. 2 (2015): 242–54.

Millar, Gearoid. "Investing in Peace? Foreign Direct Investment as Economic Justice in Sierra Leone." *Third World Quarterly* 36, no. 9 (2015): 1700–16.

Millar, Gearoid. "Local Experiences of Liberal Peace: Marketization and Emerging Conflict Dynamics in Sierra Leone." *Journal of Peace Research* 53, no. 4 (2016): 569–81.

Millar, Gearoid. "Respecting Complexity: Compound Friction and Unpredictability in Peacebuilding," in *Peacebuilding and Friction: Global and Local Encounters in Post-conflict Societies*, eds. Annika Björkdahl, Kristine Höglund, Gearoid Millar, Jair van der Lijn, and Willemijn Verkoren, 32–47. London: Routledge, 2016.

Millar, Gearoid. *Ethnographic Peace Research: Approaches and Tensions*. Basingstoke: Palgrave, 2018.

Millar, Gearoid. "Coopting Authority and Privatizing Force in Rural Africa: Ensuring Corporate Power over Land and People." *Rural Sociology* (In Press).

Millar, Gearoid, Jair van der Lijn, and Willemijn Verkoren. "Peacebuilding Plans and Local Reconfigurations: Frictions between Imported Processes and Indigenous Practices." *International Peacekeeping* 20, no. 2 (2013): 137–43.

Mosse, David. "The Anthropology of International Development." *Annual Review of Anthropology* 42 (2013): 227–46.

Müller, Tanya R., and Zuhair Bashar. "'UNAMID is Just Like Clouds in Summer, They Never Rain': Local Perceptions of Conflict and the Effectiveness of UN Peacekeeping Missions". *International Peacekeeping* 24, no. 5 (2017): 756–79.

Murphy, William P. "The Sublime Dance of Mende Politics: An African Aesthetic of Charismatic Power." *American Ethnologist* 25, no. 4 (1998): 563–82.

Nordstrom, Carolyn. *Shadows of War: Power and International Profiteering in the Twenty-First Century*. Berkeley: University of California Press, 2004.

Nordstrom, Carolyn and Antonius C.G.M. Robben. *Fieldwork under Fire: Contemporary Studies of Violence and Survival*. Berkeley: University of California Press, 1995.

OECD. "Evaluating Peacebuilding Activities in Settings of Conflict and Fragility: Improving Learning for Results." DAC Guidelines and Reference Series. OECD Publishing, 2012. www.oecd.org/officialdocuments/publicdisplaydocumentpdf/?cote=DCD/DAC(2012)40/FINAL&docLanguage=En (accessed October 13, 2016).

Okely, Judith. *Anthropological Practice: Fieldwork and the Ethnographic Method*. London: Berg, 2012.

Olsen, Tricia D., Leigh A. Payne, and Andrew Reiter. *Transitional Justice in Balance: Comparing Processes, Weighting Efficacy*. Washington, DC: United States Institute of Peace.

O'Neal, John R., Frances H. O'Neal, Zeev Moaz, and Bruce Russett. "The Liberal Peace: Interdependence, Democracy, and International Conflict, 1950–85." *Journal of Peace Research* 33, no. 1 (1996): 11–28.

Paffenholz, Thania, and Christoph Spurk. "Civil Society, Civil Engagement, and Peacebuilding." Social Development Papers: Conflict, Development and Reconstruction, Paper No. 36. Washington, DC: The World Bank, October 2006. www.siteresources.worldbank.org/INTCPR/Resources/WP36_web.pdf (accessed October 13, 2016).

Paffenholz, Thania, Mahammed Abu-Nimer and Erin McCandless. eds. "Peacebuilding and Development: Integrated Approaches to Evaluation." *International Journal of Peacebuilding and Development* (Special Issue) 2, no. 2 (2005): 1–5.

Paris, Roland. "Peacebuilding and the Limits of Liberal Internationalism." *International Security* 22, no. 2 (1997): 54–89.

Paris, Roland. "International Peacebuilding and the 'Mission Civilisatrice'." *Review of International Studies* 28, no. 4 (2002): 637–56.

Paris, Roland. *At War's End: Building Peace after Civil Conflict*. Cambridge: Cambridge University Press, 2004.

Paris, Roland. "Saving Liberal Peacebuilding." *Review of International Studies* 36, no. 2 (2010): 337–65.

Park, Rebekah. *The Reappeared: Argentine Former Political Prisoners*. New Burnswich: Rutgers University Press, 2014.

Pels, Peter. "What has Anthropology Learned from the Anthropology of Colonialism." *Social Anthropology* 16, no. 3 (2008): 280–99.

Peters, Krijn, and Paul Richards. "'Why We Fight': Voices of Youth Combatants in Sierra Leone." *Africa* 68, no. 2 (1998): 183–210.

Pouligny, Béatrice. "Civil Society and Post-conflict Peacebuilding: Ambiguities of International Programmes Aimed at Building 'New' Societies." *Security Dialogue* 36, no. 4 (2005): 495–510.

Pugh, Michael, Neil Cooper, and Jonathan Goodhand. *War Economies in a Regional Context: Challenges of Transformation.* London: Lynne Rienner, 2004.

Richards, Paul. *Fighting for the Rain Forest: War, Youth & Resources in Sierra Leone.* Portsmouth: Heinemann, 1996.

Richmond, Oliver P. "Resistance and the Post-liberal Peace." *Millennium: Journal of International Studies* 38, no. 3 (2010): 665–92.

Richmond, Oliver P., Annika Björkdahl, and Stefanie Kappler. "The Emerging EU Peacebuilding Framework: Confirming or Transcending Liberal Peacebuilding?" *Cambridge Review of International Affairs* 24, no. 3 (2011): 449–69.

Robben, Antonius C.G.M. "Anthropology and the Iraq War: An Uncomfortable Engagement". *Anthropology Today* 25, no. 1 (2009): 1–3.

Robben, Antonius C.G.M., and Jeffrey A. Sluka. "Fieldwork in Cultural Anthropology: An Introduction," in *Ethnographic Fieldwork: An Anthropological Reader*, eds. Antonius C.G.M. Robben and Jeffrey A. Sluka, 1–33. Malden: Wiley-Blackwell, 2012.

Rosaldo, Renato. "Grief and a Headhunter's Rage," in *Death, Mourning, and Burial: A Cross-cultural Reader*, ed. Antonius C.G.M. Robben, 167–78. Malden: Blackwell, 2014.

Sawyer, Amos. "Violent Conflicts and Governance Challenges in West Africa: The Case of the Mano River Basin Area." *Journal of Modern African Studies* 42, no. 3 (2004): 437–63.

Sawyer, Edward. "Remove or Reform? A Case for (Restructuring) Chiefdom Governance in Post-conflict Sierra Leone." *African Affairs* 107, no. 428 (2008): 387–403.

Sending, Ole Jocob. "Why Peacebuilders Fail to Secure Ownership and be Sensitive to Context." NUPI Working Paper 755. Oslo: Norwegian Institute for International Affairs, 2009.

Shaw, Rosalind. "Rethinking Truth and Reconciliation Commissions: Lessons from Sierra Leone." USIP Report 130, 2005. www.usip.org/sites/default/files/sr130.pdf (accessed October 13, 2016).

Shaw, Rosalind. "Memory Frictions: Localizing the Truth and Reconciliation Commission in Sierra Leone." *International Journal of Transitional Justice* 1, no. 2 (2007): 183–207.

Sikkink, Kathryn, and Carrie Booth Walling. "The Impact of Human Rights Trials in Latin America." *Journal of Peace Research* 44, no. 4 (2007): 427–45.

Souva, Mark, and Brandon Prins. "The Liberal Peace Revisited: The Role of Democracy, Dependence, and Development in Militarized Interstate Dispute Initiation, 1950–1999." *International Interactions* 32, no. 2 (2006): 183–200.

Stedman, Stephen John. "The New Interventionists." *Foreign Affairs* 72, no. 1 (1992/1993): 1–16.

Tardy, Thierry. "A Critique of Robust Peacebuilding in Contemporary Peace Operations." *International Peacekeeping* 18, no. 2 (2011): 152–67.

Theidon, Kimberly. *Intimate Enemies: Violence and Reconciliation in Peru.* Philadelphia: University of Pennsylvania Press, 2013.

Tschirgi, Necla, and Cedric de Coning. "Ensuring Sustainable Peace: Strengthening Global Security and Justice through the UN Peacebuilding Architecture." Background Paper for the Commission on Global Security, Justice & Governance, 2015. www.stimson.org/sites/default/files/Commission_BP_Tschirgi_De-Coning.pdf (accessed October 13, 2016).

Tsing, Anna Lowenhaupt. *Friction: An Ethnography of Global Connection.* Princeton, NJ: Princeton University Press, 2005.

UN. "Monitoring Peace Consolidation: United Nations Practitioners" Guide to Benchmarking." 2010. www.un.org/en/peacebuilding/pbso/pdf/monitoring_peace_consolidation.pdf (accessed October 13, 2016).

US State Department. "Sierra Leone 2015 Human Rights Report: Executive Summary". 2015. www.state.gov/documents/organization/252937.pdf (accessed May 29, 2017).

Van Leeuwen, Mathijs. *Partners in Peace; Discourses and Practices of Civil-Society Peacebuilding.* Aldershot: Ashgate, 2009.

Van Tongeren, Paul, Malin Brenk, Marte Hellema, and Juliette Verhoeven. *People Building Peace II: Successful Stories of Civil Society.* Utrecht: European Centre for Conflict Prevention, 2005.

Vigh, Henrik. *Navigating Terrains of War: Youth and Soldiering in Guinea-Bissau.* New York: Berghahn Books, 2006.

Vrasti, Wanda. "The Strange Case of Ethnography and International Relations." *Millennium* 37, no. 2 (2008): 279–301.

Wallensteen, Peter, and Margareta Sollenberg. "After the Cold War: Emerging Patterns of Armed Conflict 1989–94." *Journal of Peace Research* 32, no. 3 (1995): 345–60.

WHO. *World Health Statistics 2010.* Geneva: WHO Press, 2010.

Williams, Paul D. "The Peace and Security Council of the African Union: Evaluating an Embryonic International Institution." *The Journal of Modern African Studies* 47, no. 4 (2009): 603–26.

Witter, Sophie, Haja Wurie, and Maria Paola Bertone. "The Free Health Care Initiative: How has it Affected Health Workers in Sierra Leone?" *Health Policy and Planning* 31, no. 1 (2016): 1–9.

Young, Crawford. "The Heart of the African Conflict Zone: Democratization, Ethnicity, Civil Conflict, and the Great Lakes Crisis." *Annual Review of Political Science* 9 (2006): 301–28.

Zoomers, Annelies. "Globalisation and the Foreignisation of Space: Seven Processes Driving the Current Global Land Grab." *Journal of Peasant Studies* 37, no. 2 (2010): 429–47.

Suspicion and Ethnographic Peace Research (Notes from a Local Researcher)

Nerve Valerio Macaspac

ABSTRACT

In this article, I focus upon the notion of suspicion as a lens to better understand the distinct challenges that local researchers from the Global South encounter in ethnographic fieldwork when studying peace and peacebuilding in the context of active armed conflict within their countries. Over the last decade, scholars have increasingly deployed ethnographic approaches to better understand peacebuilding, devoting careful attention to local actors and processes that shape the practices and outcomes of international peacebuilding efforts in post-conflict environments in the Global South. While this local turn in Peace Research has led towards a renewed awareness of the challenges in ethnographic fieldwork in situations of war, armed conflict and political violence, most of the conversations in the emergent Ethnographic Peace Research (EPR) literature focus upon and draw from the experiences of researchers from the Global North who conduct ethnographic research in the Global South. Begging to be considered in the EPR literature are the experiences of local researchers from the Global South who are immersed in ethnographic research in their countries, and what these experiences tell us about the differential politics in ethnographic research.

I. Introduction

'Do not to talk to that person in the camouflage short pants,' my local research assistant in the field tells me as we pass by the municipal police station. Not knowing how to respond to this unexpected implicit warning, I do not say anything and maintain my pace. As I continue to walk, I turn my eye slightly to the left to try to get a glimpse of the person being referred to. I see a figure wearing a plain, white, round-neck T-shirt and camouflage short pants. I have been in this municipality of mostly indigenous peoples in the northern part of the Philippines for a month now. In the late 1980s, community leaders and members declared a ban on the entry of the Philippine military and the Maoist insurgent group, the New People's Army (NPA). I have been conducting interviews about the ways the community legitimizes and enforces the ban, protecting civilian lives from the impact of almost five decades of on-going armed conflict.

It is now approaching 5 pm on a weekday in August 2014. The rain has stopped after a downpour throughout the day, and the main road that leads

---

This article was originally published with error. This version has been corrected. Please see Corrigendum (http://dx.doi.org/10.1080/13533312.2018.1493773)

to the *poblacion,* the municipal town center, is busy with the arrival of two public jeepneys, stopping in front of the Municipal Hall. Fifteen to twenty passengers, older men and women and young adults, slowly disembark from each jeepney, each carrying a shopping bag or a daypack, returning after a daytrip from a neighboring municipality. Across the Municipal Hall, in front of a newly constructed shopping mall, children as young as seven years old wearing their school uniforms, carrying backpacks and holding umbrellas walk on the road in pairs or groups after being dismissed from the nearby elementary school. A couple of government employees are coming out of the Municipal Hall, crossing the road to stop by the public market to buy some produce before walking home. A number of community residents, mostly men, are passing time outside the shopping mall – sitting, standing, squatting, chewing *moma* (betel nut), talking to each other – observing the 'scene' at the jeepney terminal, Municipal Hall, public market, and police station.

The police station is a one-story structure, sandwiched between the public market to the right and a two-story shopping complex to the left. The location of the police station – built in the middle of two structures frequented daily by local traders, farmers, store owners, shoppers, children – is strategic. Since the 1980s, municipal police stations in the interior rural parts of many provinces in the Philippines have often been targets of sniping and raids by members of the NPA, a rebel armed group waging the world's longest communist insurgency led by the Communist Party of the Philippines (CPP). Armed attacks by the rebels are meant to harass state security agents, secure firearms and ammunitions, or punish 'counter-revolutionary' police officers. In establishing a police station right between two public spaces frequented by civilians, the municipal police force looks after its security by making it difficult for rebels to attack the station by mobilizing a net of civilian informants in the area that could track rebel movements and alert the police officers ahead of time. Likewise, rebels find it challenging to conduct armed activities near the presence of civilians fearing casualties will result in anger and isolation from the communities that they rely on for support.

I am now thirty feet away from the police station, moving from north to south, walking towards the public market. I approach a spot where I am directly parallel to where the person wearing camouflage short pants is standing. 'That person is suspected as an intelligence agent,' my research assistant continues with the warning. I do not respond nor do I turn my head to look at the person's face. I do not want to in case we lock eyes with each other. I move as indifferently as possible, not wanting to attract attention. I am aware that most of the people hanging out in the *poblacion* know that I am not from here, a place where everyone is related to everybody. My casual urban clothes signal that I am possibly from Manila, one of the many tourists from the lowlands who come here for a couple of days to experience the cool mountain climate and get a glimpse of the indigenous ways of life. My research assistant quietly walks with me. I find a series of questions spinning through my head: Would it be better if I turn to recognize the person's face? How important is this moment in my ethnography? Should I worry about my security? Does my research assistant feel some form of validation or anxiety for sharing a 'village secret' with me? What if the person knows what my research assistant alleges? And what if the person knows that I know the allegation? What if the person knows that I have been asking questions to community residents about

the armed conflict and the ways in which the community responds to the violence? What if, in turn, I become the object of suspicion? What are the stakes?
From where I am, it will take one minute to enter and exit the person's line of
sight. I maintain my pace and kept walking.

I highlight this moment in my fieldwork as a doctoral student from the Philippines to focus upon the notion of suspicion as a lens to understand the distinct challenges that local researchers from the Global South encounter in
ethnographic fieldwork when studying peace and peacebuilding in the
context of active armed conflict within their home countries. Over the last
decade, scholars have increasingly deployed ethnographic approaches to
better understand peacebuilding, devoting careful attention to local actors
and processes that shape the practices and outcomes of international peacebuilding efforts in post-conflict environments in the Global South.[1] While
this local turn[2] in Peace Research (PR) has led towards a renewed awareness
of the challenges to ethnographic fieldwork in situations of war, armed conflict and political violence, most of the conversations in the emergent Ethnographic Peace Research (EPR) literature focus upon and draw from the
experiences of researchers from the Global North who conduct ethnographic
research in the Global South. Begging to be considered in the EPR literature
are the experiences of local researchers from the Global South who are
immersed in ethnographic research in their home countries, and what these
experiences tell us about the differential politics in ethnographic research.

Scholars have acknowledged the ways in which researchers often become
an object of suspicion. Jeffrey Sluka argued that suspicion is among the
main sources of danger in ethnographic fieldwork, noting that almost every
anthropologist has encountered being suspected as spies.[3] In the context of
an active armed conflict, researchers oftentimes face being suspected by competing armed actors. Nancy Howell posited that researchers who study insurgency and counterinsurgency were often suspected by military officials of
supporting the rebels and by the rebels of spying for the government or competing for public support.[4] While suspicion as a social process is common to
ethnographic fieldwork, and particularly so in the context of armed conflict, I
argue that the ways in which one becomes an object of suspicion and the consequences of suspicion vary between local researchers from the Global South
and researchers from the Global North. Local researchers are easily perceived
as politically biased or lacking neutrality by state and non-state armed actors
because of their personal or professional relationships and political

---

[1]See, for instance, Millar, *Ethnographic Approach to Peacebuilding*; Moore, *Peacebuilding Practices in Two Bosnian Towns*; and Autesserre, *Peaceland*.

[2]For a discussion of the local turn in Peace Research, see Autesserre, "Going Micro"; Mac Ginty, "Indigenous Peace-Making Versus the Liberal Peace"; Mac Ginty, *International Peacebuilding and Local Resistance*; and Richmond and Mitchell, *Hybrid Forms of Peace*.

[3]Sluka, "Introduction."

[4]Howell, *Surviving Fieldwork*.

involvement. If suspected as spies, the consequences can be severe and long-term, even beyond the tenure of their fieldwork. By virtue of citizenship, local researchers from the Global South are subject to national and local laws, security policies and state surveillance in their countries. They can be subjected to vilification, intimidation and physical harm. Their current or future professional careers can be jeopardized if they intend to live and work in their countries.

Further, drawing from my experiences as a doctoral student from the Philippines who is trained in the US, I also argue that local researchers who are trained in the Global North and who conduct ethnographic research in their countries in the Global South experience 'double suspicion'. Double suspicion refers to processes through which local researchers encounter suspicion simultaneously from the local communities they work with, who tend to be suspicious of Western perspectives about the Global South, on the one hand, and from the community of scholars in the Global North who perceive a lack of scholarly distance from local researchers who conduct research in their home countries.

This article provides a reflective account of fieldwork experiences from one local researcher from the Global South. Such accounts are much needed, the paper argues, to better capture the wide range of challenges faced by EPR in studying peace and peacebuilding. With most armed conflicts occurring in the Global South,[5] local researchers are often better positioned to ethnographically investigate the processes through which sustainable and culturally relevant peace can emerge within their countries in relation to broader global political realities. They are often well equipped to immerse themselves in long-term ethnographic research and examine local actors and processes with the breadth and depth of their understanding of local norms, customs and histories, their high-level language capabilities, and extensive personal and professional connections necessary to succeed in the field. However, local researchers also face many challenges, including suspicion and the consequences of suspicion, which are not addressed in existing EPR literature. Additionally, many of the recommendations for how to navigate the risks and dangers of ethnographic fieldwork draw from the experiences of researchers from the Global North that do not necessarily apply to local researchers from the Global South.

In the first part of the article, I examine the key differences of the experiences and consequences of suspicion between local researchers and their foreign counterparts from the Global North. In the second part, I explore the notion of double suspicion that local researchers who are trained in universities in the Global North navigate, touching upon issues of engaged scholarship, ethnographic reflexivity and whiteness. To examine the processes of

---

[5]Pettersson and Wallensteen, "Armed Conflicts, 1946–2014."

both suspicion and double suspicion, I include vignettes of my dissertation fieldwork experience as a doctoral student in the US from the Philippines. In my dissertation, I examine the work required from civilian communities in making peace beyond the purview of the state through an investigation of the phenomenon of self-organized and community-led peace zones (popularly understood as demilitarized geographic areas) in the Philippines against a backdrop of nearly five decades of armed conflict between the state and a Maoist rebel organization. These vignettes reflect upon my experiences as a local researcher engaged in EPR, focusing upon suspicion and double suspicion as challenges I encounter in and out of the field site. I then conclude this article by offering a summary of my arguments and sharing insights on key topics for related future studies that can assist local researchers from the Global South in preparing and planning to engage in EPR in their countries.

II. Suspicion

I never had an interview or engagement with the person that my research assistant was referring to. While I took note of the warning from my research assistant in my head notes and field journal, I did not end up pursuing the story. At that particular moment, it was my intention to hold off from probing the circumstances of the person in question as well as the reasons behind my research assistant's warning. My inaction could be viewed as a missed opportunity to pursue potentially valuable information. It could also be perceived as a lapse in judgment in terms of my own security in the field: for the more we know, after all, the better we can assess the full risk, plan ahead, and pre-empt any possible harm to ourselves and our interlocutors. I thought about these concerns while in the field, but held back from asking questions to my research assistant or looking for information that could shed light on the identity and activities of the person in question. I did not pursue this line of inquiry due to concern that it would circulate in the community. The risks for a local researcher asking about a community member who is suspected of being an intelligence agent could easily slide into a scenario where I might in turn be made into an object of suspicion: Why is he interested to know more about this individual? For what purpose does he want to know? Who does he work for? I returned to the field in the summer of 2016. After catching up with some of my interlocutors, I was able to verify news about an incident a year before when members of the NPA ambushed a resident within the municipality during a town fiesta. The target of the ambush survived multiple gunshot wounds and has since left the municipality. During an interview with a community leader about the incident, I found out that the person who was ambushed is the same person my research assistant warned me about.

From insurgency and counterinsurgency to the 'global war on terror', suspicion has different iterations and becomes a part of daily life among civilian communities entangled in armed conflict. State security forces and non-state armed groups are intensely concerned with determining whether or not civilians support the 'enemy'. Meanwhile, civilians are often suspicious of each other for sympathizing, aiding or working on behalf of either of the armed groups to the detriment of the community. Civilians who have been suspected often face political vilification, discrimination, isolation, arrest, harassment, physical harm and elimination through extrajudicial assassination. Julianna Ochs defines objects of suspicion as those 'forbidden to approach'.[6] In Northern Ireland, many individuals were placed under arrest on the basis of being suspected as an IRA member, with suspicion giving rise to derogatory and discriminatory laws and military control of the population.[7] Over 3000 people were arrested in Nepal on the basis of suspicion regarding their membership of or sympathy for the Communist Party of Nepal (CPN) after the state declared a state of emergency in 2002.[8] Judith Pettigrew also witnessed civilians who were suspected to be rebel sympathizers hit with rifles by members of the Nepali military.[9] In the Philippines, many indigenous peoples who were suspected of being Maoist sympathizers were disappeared or killed by armed groups operating clandestinely.[10] Through these processes, suspicion works to control the civilian population on a daily basis by generating a constant sense of fear and anxiety.

In insurgency and counterinsurgency, the precarity of daily life and competing political and military agendas of state and non-state armed actors generate uncertainty and ambivalence among civilian communities entangled in armed conflicts. Pettigrew's ethnography of the violent conflict between Maoist insurgents of the CPN and the Royal Nepalese Army captures this well:

> While the security forces were in the village, people feared that the army would learn about their interactions with the Maoists. When the army left, villagers worried that the Maoists would interpret their interactions with the army as treacherous.[11]

Pettigrew also observes that suspicion replaced the openness of community life when residents were accused of taking sides.[12] Armed groups were also suspicious of community assemblies for grassroots development in rural areas, accusing community residents of supporting the other side.[13] In Northern Ireland, Paddy Hillyard notes that the Catholic Irish became a 'suspect community' for the British, who viewed every Irish person as a potential IRA supporter at the height of British counterinsurgency.[14] In the Philippines,

---

[6]Ochs, *Security and Suspicion*, 81.
[7]Bigo and Guittet, "Northern Island as Metaphor."
[8]Pettigrew, "Living Between the Maoists."
[9]Pettigrew, Shneiderman, and Harper, "Relationships, Complicity and Representation."
[10]Stavenhagen, "Special Rapporteur on Indigenous People."
[11]Pettigrew, Shneiderman, and Harper, "Relationships, Complicity and Representation," 23.
[12]Pettigrew, "Living Between the Maoists."
[13]Rechlin et al., "*Lal Salam* and *Hario Ban*."
[14]Hillyard, *Suspect Community*.

state security forces label indigenous people's communities as 'hotbeds of ter-rorism', and identify many indigenous peoples' leaders as suspected commu-nist sympathizers.[15]

Several anthropologists have discussed the ways in which researchers encounter suspicion in the field. Nancy Howell observes that in an insurgency and counterinsurgency, the military may suspect anthropologists of support-ing the rebels while the rebels may suspect anthropologists of working for the government.[16] John Borneman also suggests that the presence of researchers often provokes suspicion among our interlocutors out of fear that the former will use the information to betray the latter.[17] Jeffrey Sluka avers that every anthropologist who has done fieldwork has been suspected as a spy for a number of reasons, many of which are contextual.[18] In the early decades of the discipline of anthropology in the nineteenth century, the suspicion of anthropologists over possibilities of their collaboration with authority reflected the power relations during the colonial period.[19] During the first world war, Franz Boas revealed that at least four anthropologists worked as spies for the US government.[20] Throughout the cold war, anthropologists conducting fieldwork abroad were suspected as spies amidst the deployment of intelligence agents by the US government in many countries around the world. Suspicion of anthropologists continues particularly in the context of the 'global war on terror' post-9/11.[21]

Risk and danger are inherent in the ethnographic field process.[22] While scholars reveal a wide range of sources of suspicion in ethnographic fieldwork, I argue that local researchers from the Global South who conduct research in their countries experience the consequences of suspicion differently than their foreign counterparts from the Global North. Local researchers who study war and peace in their countries of origin often draw from the reflections of their foreign counterparts when preparing for potential challenges, risks and dangers of ethnographic fieldwork. However, local researchers will realize that they do not carry many of the privileges of their foreign colleagues when navigating difficult situations in the field. Further, many of the rec-ommendations that foreign researchers propose in navigating physical, emotional, ethical and professional challenges in the field emerge from experi-ences, reflections and recommendations of mostly foreign researchers that often are inadequate or not applicable to the experiences of local researchers as citizens of the countries they study. Writing about the experiences of local

---

[15]Chua, "Bloodshed and the Coercive Communal Peace."
[16]Howell, *Surviving Fieldwork*.
[17]Borneman, "Fieldwork Experience, Collaboration, and Interlocution," 238.
[18]Sluka, "Reflections on Managing Danger in Fieldwork."
[19]Ibid., 240.
[20]Boas, "Scientists as Spies."
[21]Borneman, "Fieldwork Experience, Collaboration, and Interlocution."
[22]Peterson, "Sheer Foolishness."

researchers is a difficult task. I am aware of the risks of essentializing local or foreign researchers or deploying simplistic binaries in comparing the experiences of local researchers from the Global South and foreign researchers from the Global North. This is not my intent. Rather, my aim is to better understand the challenges of EPR that local researchers face in their countries.

I suggest two key differences in the consequences of suspicion for local researchers immersed in ethnographic fieldwork in their countries in the Global South relative to their foreign counterparts from the Global North. First, local researchers oftentimes are deemed by armed actors as expendable lives. They also often become objects of suspicion because of their family and personal relationships, previous professional background or political involvement and so can more easily be perceived as politically biased or lacking neutrality by local armed groups than foreign, and particularly white, researchers. The consequences of being suspected as a spy can be severe for local researchers. By virtue of their citizenship, they are subject to national and local laws, security policies and state surveillance, which can result in vilification, harassment, intimidation, disappearance or death. One example of this is Myrna Mack, a UK-trained Maya-Chinese Guatemalan anthropologist, who was stabbed to death by a low-ranking security official in 1990. Mack studied the social upheaval, displacement and human rights violations experienced by the indigenous Maya during the insurgency and counterinsurgency in Guatemala. Over 100 university professors and researchers have been murdered since the 1980s, with many more going into exile over this time.[23]

In the Philippines, where political authorities and armed actors are regarded by human rights organizations as having impunity from punishment for the extrajudicial killings and disappearances of perceived dissidents as well as members of the local political opposition, media, NGOs and academics,[24] local researchers who are involved in political movements often receive direct threats of harm and are harassed through overt forms of surveillance that are meant to intimidate.[25] For instance, while conducting research about the militarization of indigenous peoples communities in Mindanao, Filipino anthropologists and university professors Myfel Paluga and Andrea Malaya Ragragio observed pairs of men on motorcycles following them,[26] a mode of surveillance that commonly preceded the disappearance and extrajudicial killings of many academics and activists. Meanwhile, the circumstances are oftentimes different for foreign researchers from the Global North. For instance, in Nepal when Maoist insurgents were making anti-foreign statements and forcing foreign development workers to leave the areas with strong rebel

---

[23]Oglesby, "Myrna Mack," 256.
[24]See, for instance, Human Rights Watch, "Philippines": Amnesty International, "Philippines: Above the Law"; Alston, "Promotion and Protection of All Human Rights."
[25]Tolentino and Raymundo, Kontra-Gahum.
[26]Saligumba, "Two UP Profs Assail Surveillance."

influence, anthropologist Sara Shneiderman received a hand delivered message from Maoist insurgents to notify her that she was under surveillance and to order her to leave the local community where she was conducting research.[27] One source of the different consequences of suspicion for local and foreign researchers is that state or non-state armed actors are more calculating when they approach the latter, noting the repercussions that could emerge from a controversy over placing a foreign researcher in danger, including changes in the conflict environment or impact to an ongoing peace process.

A second key difference in the consequences of suspicion to local and foreign researchers involves mobility. Scholars have suggested some of the ways to mitigate security concerns and dangers in high-risk ethnographic fieldwork including occasionally leaving the field site,[28] conducting multisite ethnography, and shorter periods of data collection to avoid attracting suspicion from armed actors.[29] Other scholars also recommend to 'flee' the field site when necessary.[30] However, moving and travelling amidst a high-risk conflict is not easy for local researchers. Leaving the conflict area poses difficult challenges including crossing checkpoints, being trailed by informants or security forces, or being forcibly disappeared. If they are able to flee the field site, leaving the country may not be as easy as it is likely to be for their foreign counterparts. Researchers from the Global North have a relative ease of movement and travel in many developing countries, a privilege and 'double standard' that Mack observed as their 'risk-free access even to the remotest regions'.[31] Without discounting the circumstances wherein foreign researchers experience security risks in the field as a result of being foreign or white in a developing country – as Sally Moore notes of the difficulty in making oneself as inconspicuous as possible when 'there is no way that a white person can be inconspicuous in an African country'[32] – researchers from the Global North can rely on relatively less impinged mobility in the Global South.

Such ease of movement is useful when the time comes that foreign researchers need to flee the field site and the country they are in. Many researchers from the Global North have noted the wonders that American, Canadian or European passports can do to protect their lives in the most challenging situations, but being white also renders one the advantage of getting through borders. This is highlighted in the experience of Nasser Abufarha, a Palestinian-American anthropologist who conducted research on 'suicide

---

[27]Pettigrew, Shneiderman, and Harper, "Relationships, Complicity and Representation."
[28]See, for instance, Millar, *An Ethnographic Approach to Peacebuilding*, 129; Autesserre, *Peaceland*, 287.
[29]Pettigrew, Shneiderman, and Harper, "Relationships, Complicity and Representation," 23.
[30]Ibid., 21.
[31]Oglesby, "Myrna Mack," 255.
[32]Moore, "Encounter and Suspicion in Tanzania," 154.

bombers' in his hometown in Palestine. While Abufarha successfully navigated a border checkpoint manned by Israeli security forces by showing his US passport, he observed that he was also able to do so by crossing the border with another colleague who is white, 'one who is not an Arab like him'.[33] Additionally, for many foreign researchers from the Global North who may have encountered suspicion in the field, re-locating back to their home countries and being physically away from the field site offer a level of protection from the consequences of suspicion as well as safety in publishing ethnographic information that could be considered sensitive. Local researchers face a different scenario. Mack once commented, as recalled by Elizabeth Oglesby, that 'the difference between a US scholar and a Guatemalan scholar is that in the United States, you say "publish or perish." Here, we say, "if we publish, we perish."'[34]

III. Double suspicion

Another key way in which the experiences and consequences of suspicion are distinct for local researchers from the Global South is 'double suspicion'. Double suspicion refers to the ways in which local researchers become simultaneously suspected by their local interlocutors and the international community of scholars. The first aspect of double suspicion, of being suspected by local interlocutors, underscores the ways in which Western-educated local researchers face suspicion from local communities who are ambivalent towards the role of Western education.[35] The second aspect of double suspicion refers to the ways in which Western scholars tend to suspect the intellectual contributions of local researchers. In conducting research, local researchers from the Global South are expected to demonstrate scholarly distance and to defamiliarize their knowledge of their own countries or communities. Emerging from literary theory as a device that compels readers to 'examine their automated perceptions of that which is so familiar that it seems natural and so unquestionable',[36] social researchers have mobilized the concept of defamiliarization in fostering a capacity for experiencing a moment of 'eureka' or surprise during fieldwork, with the 'element of surprise' acknowledged as a necessary and important instigator of thought that opens up whole new horizons.[37] The framework of defamiliarization in ethnography and social research is underpinned by the notion of 'cultural blindness',[38] that if ethnographers are very familiar with the culture being studied, there is a

---

[33]Abufarha, *Making of a Human Bomb*, 116.
[34]Oglesby, "Myrna Mack," 255.
[35]Kaomea, "Dilemmas of an Indigenous Academic"; see also Smith, *Decolonizing Methodologies*; Spivak, "Can the Subaltern Speak?"
[36]Bell, Blythe, and Sengers, "Making by Making Strange," 151.
[37]Guyer, "Quickening of the Unknown," 287.
[38]Alvesson, "Culture Perspective on Organizations."

tendency to be less attentive to the banal and taken-for-granted features of the culture itself.[39]

Other scholars argue that defamiliarization is more difficult than gaining access in the field.[40] In my experience as a Filipino doctoral student in the US, I needed to learn quickly and exhaustively the ways in which Western scholars conceptualize and study the Philippines and their intellectual and methodological tools in order for me to engage the existing scholarship in the US about my home country. I also needed to learn the dominant Western paradigms that frame these scholarships that oftentimes do not have any equivalent or basis at home.[41] Further, scholars prescribe a variety of 'estrangement strategies' to help ethnographers develop a detached and 'objective' perspective when interpreting research data including physically leaving the field site and breaking intimate ties with local interlocutors.[42] These estrangement tools often counter the expectations of local communities that the relationships between local researchers and interlocutors will be enduring.[43]

Additionally, local researchers are expected to maintain 'scholarly distance'. In 2014, I applied for a research grant to study the peacebuilding approaches enacted by indigenous peoples in the Philippines post-9/11, when many indigenous communities have been militarized and hundreds of indigenous peoples were disappeared or assassinated by state security agents. I highlighted my connections to the proposed field sites, noting my previous professional work experience as an independent researcher and documentary filmmaker on indigenous peoples' rights in the Philippines. The funding organization denied my application and, upon my request, emailed a review:

> The reviewers felt that your project was very strong with a good focus on the link between indigeneity and securitization. The reviewers felt that the application demonstrated your deep involvement with the issue, which they applauded, with some concern that there was therefore little evidence of scholarly distance.[44]

In the review, 'scholarly distance' is deployed as a value opposite of 'deep involvement' where deeper political engagement signals a lack of scholarly objectivity. Scholarly distance, if read as a process of studying social phenomenon by a disengaged outsider, also is established as a favoured intellectual practice that merits greater recognition compared to a scholar's deep involvement in social issues being studied. Debates around 'engaged anthropology'

---

[39]Prasad, *Crafting Qualitative Research*, 87.
[40]Ybema and Kamsteeg, "Making the Familiar Strange."
[41]See, for instance, Heryanto, "Can There Be Southeast Asians in Southeast Asian Studies?"
[42]de Jong, Kamsteeg, and Ybema, "Ethnographic Strategies for Making the Familiar Strange," 178.
[43]Kaomea, "Dilemmas of an Indigenous Academic," 68.
[44]Email correspondence, July 2014.

have been around arguably since the emergence of the discipline, and anthropologists operationalize the notion of 'participant' in participant observation differently, with some anthropologists becoming involved in activism, policy-making or social justice advocacy while others demonstrate their engagement through teaching and public education, social critique, and participatory and collaborative social research with local communities.[45] Proponents and practitioners of engaged anthropology argue that ethnographic detachment and disengaged anthropology in the face of social injustice, wars and indigenous peoples' rights violations – among other global problems that anthropologists seek to understand – are morally and ethically unacceptable and irrelevant to current geopolitical and economic conditions of the world.[46] In this regard, local researchers from the Global South are compelled to navigate their positionality as researcher and citizen, academic and advocate, and insider and outside amidst rising human rights violations during armed conflicts. Rosa Cordillera Castillo, a Filipina anthropologist who studies the impact of the armed conflict in Mindanao, notes the difficulty in assuming a position of neutrality in the face of human misery caused by war.[47] While being in both positions of witness and researcher is oftentimes difficult for many researchers, the desire to be 'objective', 'neutral' and 'disengaged' when studying violent conflicts in their countries is often what renders local researchers objects of suspicion among the civilian communities they study.

The demands of Western academic institutions regarding scholarly distance and defamiliarization are underpinned by a claim over what comprises objective, scholarly and social scientific truth in ways that are largely predicated upon the experiences of specifically white researchers from the Global North. Additionally, while reflexivity is acknowledged as a central aspect of ethnographic research that allows for an examination of one's 'hidden preconceptions that orient social thought',[48] reflexivity is also predicated upon the contact between whiteness and white normativity[49] and the 'other'. What concerns me is how most approaches to ethnographic reflexivity set the experiences of white researchers as the dominant and universal benchmark of ethnographic discovery and objective social scientific knowledge. At the same time, reflexivity serves as a practice and cultural form that validates the white researcher's self-expression, self-discovery and self-critique, further contributing to the social reproduction

---

[45]See, for instance, Low and Merry, "Engaged Anthropology."
[46]See, for instance, Sanford and Angel-Ajani, *Engaged Observer*; Speed, "Human Rights and Anthropology"; Hale, "Activist Research vs. Cultural Critique"; and Scheper-Hughes, "The Primacy of the Ethical."
[47]Castillo, "Emotional, Political, and Analytical Labor."
[48]Emirbayer and Desmond, "Race and Reflexivity," 576.
[49]White normativity refers not only to practices and ways of thinking held by whites in which white people are the 'center of the universe', but also to the racial structures, particularly in the US, in which whites occupy 'an unquestioned and unexamined place of esteem, power, and privilege'. Bell and Hartmann, "Diversity in Everyday Discourse," 907.

and embodiment of whiteness. Local researchers are marginalized within this scheme of ethnographic knowledge production.

I belabour the ways in which the second aspect of double suspicion merits critical examination to attend to how dominant intellectual and methodological frameworks often conceal white normativity and Western-centric discourses behind a set of universal claims over objective scholarship, scientific knowledge and intellectual contributions. Attending to the double suspicion that local researchers face carries direct implications for the local and ethnographic turn in the study of peacebuilding. Critical engagement with the liberal peace framework can only go so far if its perceived limits and failures are evaluated independently from the long-term aim of social research to deconstruct, displace and disempower whiteness.[50]

IV. Conclusion

Throughout this article, I focused on suspicion as a lens to better understand the challenges of ethnographic fieldwork in the shadow of armed conflict. I argue that suspicion reveals the differential politics of danger and safety in fieldwork, illuminating our understanding of the challenges that local researchers face that are often excluded from the literature on peacebuilding. Geraldine Lee-Treweek and Stephanie Linkogle suggest that the risks researchers experience often mirror the risks faced by the communities being studied.[51] While this is true in many situations, I argue that local researchers experience danger through suspicion and its consequences differently from their foreign, specifically white, colleagues. Given that most armed conflicts today occur in developing countries and become more intense over time,[52] local researchers who study war and peace in their countries of origin are compelled more than ever to better navigate the risks and dangers associated with ethnographic fieldwork. The concept of suspicion offers pedagogic information for aspiring local researchers.

More broadly, focusing on suspicion as a danger of high-risk ethnographic fieldwork allows me to foreground a new approach towards researcher safety. Researchers and academic institutions meticulously attend to the protection of human subjects while discussions of researcher safety remain secondary. In highlighting the ways in which local researchers who study armed conflicts and peacebuilding often become objects of more intense suspicion that can result in threats to their lives, I suggest that the risks experienced by local researchers and their research interlocutors are interconnected, requiring careful attention from the researcher and research institutions. Hence, universities and research funding institutions that require detailed plans for the

---

[50]Ibid., 179.
[51]Lee-Treweek and Linkogle, *Danger in the Field*, 2.
[52]Gates, Nygård, Strand, and Urdal, *Trends in Armed Conflict*.

protection of research participants also need to develop mechanisms that address and monitor researcher safety. Academic programme and research advisers and their respective students can develop a system of reporting of researcher safety in the field, noting possible scenarios and levels of danger, ways to mitigate the challenges of fieldwork, and concrete steps that can be carried out by the university or research institutions to protect the safety of the researcher.

Further, I suggest the concept of double suspicion to better capture some of the epistemological concerns surrounding ethnography, reflexivity and positionality. I argue that local researchers experience suspicion from local interlocutors in their countries of origin who are critical of Western education and from Western academic institutions that question the contributions of local researchers. I also argue that double suspicion reveals the limits and problems of the practice of ethnography and the production of ethnographic knowledge, most notably the (un)conscious reproduction of whiteness and white normativity that often are veiled by notions of defamiliarization, scholarly distance and neutrality. The emphasis in the local and ethnographic turn within the peacebuilding literature on the phenomenon of grassroots peacebuilding, and the limits of the liberal peace agenda, is an opportunity for the interdisciplinary discipline of Peace Studies to generate a new cohort of ethnographers and social researchers, local or foreign, who can facilitate the emancipatory objectives of the study and practice of peacebuilding rooted upon the displacement and disruption of whiteness and white supremacy.

I suggest that suspicion as an analytical framework in EPR and as a conceptual angle in understanding war and peace needs to be taken up in future studies. Suspicion can inform ethnographers of the internal dynamics and conflicts that shape violence and peacebuilding in particular places. For instance, suspicion and its circulation as knowledge can illustrate the social contradictions within communities where a population may appear homogenous. The warning I received from my research assistant signalled how even within a community where everyone is related to each other to varying degrees, and where shared histories define their identity as indigenous peoples, there are political differences and antagonisms that are rooted less on kinship and more upon ideological and political commitments. Suspicion also is a dimension of ethnographic fieldwork that is important in understanding grassroots peacebuilding practices since it reveals the internal processes through which communities navigate the competing agendas of state and non-state armed actors.

Further, in attending to suspicion, ethnographers can better understand the precarity of the situations of everyday life in active armed conflict as well as the political processes, relationships and tensions within the communities they study. Because suspicion is a social process that is context specific, attending to the dynamics and dimensions of suspicion may allow ethnographers to produce fine-grained analysis of place-specific grassroots peacebuilding practices. Finally, suspicion can reveal the ways in which civilian communities become battlegrounds where contending claims over people's 'hearts and minds' are fought, offering insight into community-initiated negotiations over legitimacy and political power between civilians and armed actors.

Disclosure statement

No potential conflict of interest was reported by the author.

Funding

This work was supported by UCLA Geography Helin Research Travel Grant; International Peace Research Association (IPRA) Foundation Research Grant.

Bibliography

Abufarha, Nasser. *The Making of a Human Bomb: An Ethnography of Palestinian Resistance*. Durham, NC: Duke University Press, 2009.
Alston, Philip. "Promotion and Protection of All Human Rights, Civil, Political, Economic, Social and Cultural Rights, Including the Right to Development: Report of the Special Rapporteur on Extrajudicial, Summary or Arbitrary Executions, Philip Alston." April 16, 2008. https://documents-dds-ny.un.org/doc/UNDOC/GEN/G08/130/01/PDF/G0813001.pdf?OpenElement (accessed December 10, 2016).
Alvesson, Mats. "The Culture Perspective on Organizations: Instrumental Values and Basic Features of Culture." *Scandinavian Journal of Management* 5 (1989): 123–36.
Amnesty International. "Philippines: Above the Law." December 4, 2014. www.amnestyusa.org/sites/default/files/asa_350072014.pdf (accessed December 10, 2016).
Autesserre, Severine. "Going Micro: Emerging and Future Peacekeeping Research." *International Peacekeeping* 21 (2014): 492–500. doi:10.1080/13533312.2014.950884.
Autesserre, Severine. *Peaceland: Conflict Resolution and the Everyday Politics of International Intervention*. New York: Cambridge University Press, 2014.
Bell, Genevieve, Mark Blythe, and Phoebe Sengers. "Making by Making Strange: Defamiliarization and the Design of Domestic Technologies." *ACM Transactions on Computer-Human Interaction* 12 (2005): 149–73.
Bell, Joyce M., and Douglas Hartmann. "Diversity in Everyday Discourse: The Cultural Ambiguities and Consequences of 'Happy Talk'." *American Sociological Review* 72 (2007): 895–914.

Bigo, Didier, and Emmanuel-Pierre Guittet. "Northern Island as Metaphor: Exception, Suspicion and Radicalization in the 'War on Terror'." *Security Dialogue* 42 (2011): 483–98.

Boas, Franz. "Scientists as Spies." In *To See Ourselves: Anthropology and Modern Social Issues*, ed. Thomas Weaver, 51–2. Glencoe, IL: Scott, Foresman, 1973.

Bonilla Silva, Eduardo. "Rethinking Racism." *American Sociological Review* 62 (1997): 456–79.

Bonilla Silva, Eduardo. *White Supremacy and Racism in the Post-Civil Rights Era.* Boulder, CO: Lynne Rienner, 2001.

Bonilla Silva, Eduardo. *Racism Without Racists: Color-Blind Racism and the Persistence of Racial Inequality in the United States.* Lanham, MD: Roman and Littlefield, 2003.

Borneman, John. "Fieldwork Experience, Collaboration, and Interlocution: The 'Metaphysics of Presence' in Encounters with the Syrian Mukhabarat." In *Being There: The Fieldwork Encounter and the Making of Truth*, ed. John Borneman and Abdellah Hammoudi, 237–58. Berkeley: University of California Press, 2009.

Castillo, Rosa Cordillera. "The Emotional, Political, and Analytical Labor of Engaged Anthropology Amidst Violent Political Conflict." *Medical Anthropology* 34 (2015): 70–83. doi:10.1080/01459740.2014.960564.

Chua, Peter. "Bloodshed and the Coercive Communal Peace Negotiations." In *Kontra-Gahum: Academics Against Political Killings*, ed. Rolando Tolentino and Sarah Raymundo, 42–57. Quezon City: UP Press, 2006.

de Jong, Machteld, Frans Kamsteeg, and Sierk Ybema. "Ethnographic Strategies for Making the Familiar Strange: Struggling with 'Distance' and 'Immersion' among Moroccan-Dutch Students." *Journal of Business Anthropology* 2 (2013): 168–86.

Emirbayer, Mustafa, and Matthew Desmond. "Race and Reflexivity." *Ethnic and Racial Studies* 35 (2012): 574–99.

Fanon, Franz. *The Wretched of the Earth.* New York: Grove Press, 1963.

Frankenberg, Ruth. *White Women, Race Matters: The Social Construction of Whiteness.* Minneapolis: University of Minnesota Press, 1993.

Gabriel, John. "Whiteness: Endangered Knowledges, Endangered Species?" In *Danger in the Field: Risk and Ethics in Social Research*, ed. Geraldine Lee-Treweek and Stephanie Linkogle, 168–80. London: Routledge, 2000.

Gates, Scott, Håvard Mokleiv Nygård, Håvard Strand, and Henrik Urdal. *Trends in Armed Conflict, 1946–2014.* Oslo: PRIO, 2016.

Guyer, Jane I. "The Quickening of the Unknown: Epistemologies of Surprise in Anthropology." *HAU: Journal of Ethnographic Theory* 3 (2013): 283–307. doi:10.14318/hau3.3.012.

Hancock, Black Hawk. "Steppin' Out of Whiteness." *Ethnography* 6 (2005): 427–61.

Heryanto, Ariel. "Can There Be Southeast Asians in Southeast Asian Studies?" In *Knowing Southeast Asian Subjects*, ed. Laurie J. Sears, 75–108. Seattle: University of Washington Press, 2007.

Hillyard, Paddy. *Suspect Community: People's Experience of the Prevention of Terrorism Acts in Britain.* London: Pluto, 1993.

Human Rights Watch. "Philippines: New Killings as Impunity Reigns." July 18, 2011. www.hrw.org/news/2011/07/18/philippines-new-killings-impunity-reigns (accessed December 10, 2016).

Jacobs-Huey, Lanita. "The Natives Are Gazing and Talking Back: Reviewing the Problematics of Positionality, Voice, and Accountability among 'Native'

Anthropologists." *American Anthropologist* 104, no. 3 (2002): 791–804. www.jstor. org/stable/3567257.

Kaomea, Julie. "Dilemmas of an Indigenous Academic: A Native Hawaiian Story." *Contemporary Issues in Early Childhood* 2 (2001): 67–82.

Kovach, Margaret. *Indigenous Methodologies: Characteristics, Conversations, and Contexts.* Toronto: University of Toronto Press, 2009.

Lee-Treweek, Geraldine, and Stephanie Linkogle. *Danger in the Field: Risk and Ethics in Social Research.* London: Routledge, 2000.

Lubkemann, Stephen. *Culture in Chaos: An Anthropology of the Social Condition in War.* Chicago: University of Chicago Press, 2008.

Mac Ginty, Roger. "Indigenous Peace-Making Versus the Liberal Peace." *Cooperation and Conflict* 43 (2008): 139–63. doi:10.1177/0010836708089080.

Mac Ginty, Roger. *International Peacebuilding and Local Resistance: Hybrid Forms of Peace.* London: Palgrave Macmillan, 2011.

Millar, Gearoid. *An Ethnographic Approach to Peacebuilding: Understanding Local Experience in Transitional States.* London: Routledge, 2014.

Moore, Sally. "Encounter and Suspicion in Tanzania." In *Being There: The Fieldwork Encounter and the Making of Truth*, ed. John Borneman and Abdellah Hammoudi, 151–82. Berkeley: University of California Press, 2009.

Moore, Adam. *Peacebuilding Practices in Two Bosnian Towns.* Ithaca, NY: Cornell University Press, 2013.

Narayan, Kirin. "How Native Is a 'Native' Anthropologist?" *American Anthropologist*, New Series 95, no. 3 (1993): 671–86. www.jstor.org/stable/679656.

Nordstrom, Carolyn, and Antonius Robben. *Fieldwork under Fire: Contemporary Studies of Violence and Survival.* Berkeley: University of California Press, 1995.

Ochs, Julianna. *Security and Suspicion: An Ethnography of Everyday Life in Israel.* Philadelphia: University of Pennsylvania Press, 2011.

Oglesby, Elizabeth. "Myrna Mack." In *Fieldwork under Fire: Contemporary Studies of Violence and Survival*, ed. Carolyn Nordstrom and Antonius C. G. M. Robben, 254–9. Berkeley: University of California Press, 1995.

Ohnuki-Tierney, Emiko. "'Native' Anthropologists." *American Ethnologist* 11 (1984): 584–6. doi:10.1525/ae.1984.11.3.02a00110.

Peterson, Jeff D. "Sheer Foolishness: Shifting Definitions of Danger in Conducting and Teaching Ethnographic Field Research." In *Danger in the Field: Risk and Ethics in Social Research*, ed. Geraldine Lee-Treweek and Stephanie Linkogle, 182–96. London: Routledge, 2000.

Pettersson, There'se, and Peter Wallensteen. "Armed Conflicts, 1946–2014." *Journal of Peace Research* 52 (2015): 536–50.

Pettigrew, Judith. "Living Between the Maoists and the Army in Rural Nepal." *Himalaya, The Journal of the Association for Nepal and Himalayan Studies* 23 (2003): 9–20.

Pettigrew, Judith, Sara Shneiderman, and Ian Harper. "Relationships, Complicity and Representation: Conducting Research in Nepal During the Maoist Insurgency." *Anthropology Today* 20 (2004): 20–5. doi:10.1111/j.0268-540X.2004.00248.x.

Prasad, Pushkala. *Crafting Qualitative Research: Working in the Postpositivist Traditions.* Armonk, NY: M. E. Sharpe, 2005.

Rechlin, Michael A., William R. Burch, A. L. Hammett, Bhishma Subedi, Surya Binayee, and Indu Sapkota. "*Lal Salam* and *Hario Ban*: The Effects of the Maoist Insurgency on Community Forestry in Nepal." *Forests, Trees and Livelihoods* 17 (2007): 245–53.

Richmond, Oliver. *A Post-liberal Peace.* London: Routledge, 2011.

Richmond, Oliver, and Audra Mitchell. *Hybrid Forms of Peace: From Everyday Agency to Post-liberalism.* New York: Palgrave, 2011.

Roediger, David A. *Black on White: Black Writers on What It Means to Be White.* New York: Schocken Books, 1998.

Roediger, David A. *Colored White: Transcending the Racial Past.* Berkeley: University of California Press, 2002.

Said, Edward. *Culture and Imperialism.* London: Chatto & Windus, 1993.

Saligumba, John Rizle L. "Two UP Profs Assail Surveillance." *Davao Today*, July 12, 2014. http://davaotoday.com/main/human-rights/two-up-profs-assail-surveillance/ (accessed December 10, 2016).

Sluka, Jeffrey. "Participant Observation in Violent Social Contexts." *Human Organization* 49 (1990): 114–26.

Sluka, Jeffrey. "Reflections on Managing Danger in Fieldwork: Dangerous Anthropology in Belfast." In *Fieldwork under Fire: Contemporary Studies of Violence and Survival*, ed. Carolyn Nordstrom and Antonius C. G. M. Robben, 276–94. Berkeley: University of California Press, 1995.

Sluka, Jeffrey. "Introduction." In *Ethnographic Fieldwork: An Anthropological Reader*, 2nd ed., ed. Antonius C. G. M. Robben and Jeffrey A. Sluka, 237–43. Malden, MA: Blackwell, 2012.

Smith, Linda Tuhiwai. *Decolonizing Methodologies: Research and Indigenous Peoples.* New York: Zed Books, 1999.

Spivak, Gayatri Chakravorty. "Can the Subaltern Speak?" In *Marxism and the Interpretation of Culture*, ed. Cary Nelson and Lawrence Grossberg, 271–313. Urbana: University of Illinois Press, 1988.

Stavenhagen, Rodolfo. "Promotion and Protection of All Human Rights, Civil, Political, Economic, Social and Cultural Rights, Including the Right to Development: Report of the Special Rapporteur on the Situation of Human Rights and Fundamental Freedoms of Indigenous People, Rodolfo Stavenhagen." November 15, 2007. http://unsr.vtaulicorpuz.org/site/images/docs/annual/2007-annual-hrc-a-hrc-6-15-en.pdf (accessed December 10, 2016).

Stavenhagen, Rodolfo. "Special Rapporteur on Indigenous People Presents Report to Commission on Human Rights." April 10, 2003. www.un.org/press/en/2003/hrcn1028.doc.htm (accessed December 10, 2016).

Tolentino, Rolando B., and Sarah S. Raymundo. *Kontra-Gahum: Academics Against Political Killings.* Quezon City: UP Press, 2006.

Ybema, Sierk, and Frans Kamsteeg. "Making the Familiar Strange: A Case for Disengaged Ethnography." In *Organizational Ethnography: Studying the Complexities of Everyday Life*, ed. Sierk Ybema, Dvora Yanow, Harry Wels, and Franss Kamsteeg, 101–19. London: Sage, 2009.

Critiquing Anthropological Imagination in Peace and Conflict Studies: From Empiricist Positivism to a Dialogical Approach in Ethnographic Peace Research

Philipp Lottholz

ABSTRACT
This article seeks to show how the ethnographic peace research agenda can benefit from long-standing discussions in the anthropological literature. It sets out by arguing that the 'anthropological imagination' apparent in recent debates in peace and conflict studies is informed by an empiricist positivism that conceives of ethnography as a data-gathering tool. By drawing insights from the 'writing culture' and 'Third World feminism' debates, I will show how such empiricism was challenged and partly done away with in favour of new dialogical and collaborative approaches to knowledge production. In the second part, focussed on the context of the Kyrgyz Republic in Central Asia, I will illustrate the limits and blind spots of the prevalent empiricist approach to studying peace and conflict by showing how discourses and imaginaries of a 'culture of peace', tolerance and multiculturalism conceal forms of exclusion, marginalization and hidden conflict. I will show how my own collaborative research sheds light on community security practitioners' efforts to understand and tackle security challenges. This practico-discursive analysis exemplifies how critical ethnographic peace research can help to uncover patterns of conflict management, post-conflict governmentality, and the construction and 'othering' of group identities.

Introduction

In the effort to challenge hegemonic conceptions and policies of peacebuilding and security provision, new disciplinary approaches, methodologies and theoretical lenses have been introduced into peace and conflict studies. However, different attempts to account for the complexity of interventions, widen analytical horizons and hence make post-conflict interventions and research better reflect realities 'on the ground' have proved hard to accommodate with one another. As I will argue in this article, the reception and conceptualization of ethnography in this field is indicative of a dominance of empiricist positivism and a preference of theory building and testing over in-depth research. Based on insights from the 'writing culture' and 'Third World feminism' debates, I will show how collaborative and practice-based inquiry can help to better understand on-the-ground situations by cooperatively producing knowledge *in dialogue with*, rather than *for* supposed beneficiaries.

Different debates have challenged the conceptual apparatus of peace and conflict studies and related social science disciplines, but have not led to a significant shift in the dominance of its 'normal science' mainstream. Most recently, there has been a surge in literature that tackles the complexity and historicity of peace- and statebuilding trajectories from a sociological angle.[1] This literature is helpful in pointing out how peacebuilding missions are attempting to transplant ideal-type institutions and structures that had been built up during centuries of often violent struggles and economic accumulation; or how the practices, habitus and organizational structures of interveners – especially the bureaucracies of international organizations – preclude a successful overcoming of divisions and economic dependency of conflict-affected states.[2] While the myriad groups on the intervening end – civil and military staff in the diplomatic, administrative and aid sector – receive more academic attention,[3] 'local actors' are merely a constituent part of 'intervention society' and yet to be studied.[4] Thus, the predominant focus on interveners in this literature is ironically reflecting the very 'self-referentiality' of Western interventions initially critiqued by proponents of the sociology of international intervention themselves.[5] Scholars have also shown how peacebuilding missions, notwithstanding their frequent failure or merely 'virtual' survival, are still continuously constructed as necessary to bring peace, prosperity and development to countries beyond the industrial world.[6] The contradictory nature of the peacebuilding industry is most articulately critiqued in Denskus' claim that *Peaceland* is a 'non-place' constituted by policies, lifestyles and representation techniques, which create images of peacebuilding 'success' more than actually building peace on the ground.[7]

The exclusion of 'local voices' is a main pillar of the critique of the 'liberal peace' presented by scholars united by an interest in 'critical peacebuilding'. They argued that the ignorance of the needs and values of populations subject to post-conflict intervention had affected the impasse, if not failure,

---

[1] See, for instance, Bliesemann de Guevara, *Statebuilding*; and Distler, "Intervention as a Social Practice," 327 for an overview.
[2] Bliesemann de Guevara, *Statebuilding*.
[3] See Distler, "Intervention as a Social Practice."
[4] Ibid. The same applies to most 'everyday' and sociological analyses of intervention, such as Autesserre, *Peaceland*; Bliesemann de Guevara, *Statebuilding*.
[5] Bliesemann de Guevara, *Statebuilding*, 15–6.
[6] Autesserre, *Peaceland*; Turner and Kuhn, *Tyranny of Peace*.
[7] Denskus, "Peacebuilding," 658.

of this endeavour.[8] 'Post-liberal' and 'hybrid forms of peace' were found to be already existing as a result of the adaptation, re-configuration and inversion of 'liberal peace' templates in practice; and were used as frameworks to analyse the latter processes.[9] In these debates, often referred to as 'local turn',[10] a significant role was attributed to ethnographic methods and 'anthropological imagination'. Ethnographic explorations of post-conflict contexts have indeed indicated what an ethnographic peace research agenda could look like.[11] But overall, it can be argued that the debate on this potential synthesis has been dominated by an empiricist-positivist epistemological outlook and a universalist ontology. The focus of the field did not fundamentally shift as the developing, testing and con-testation of theories – even if 'critical' ones – superseded the in-depth study of empirical realities. Catering towards global peacebuilding policy-makers and prac-titioners – or critiquing the mainstream, orthodox approaches monopolizing this activity – has thus become the main preoccupation of the 'peace writing industry' and distracted it from engaging with the struggles of people affected by conflict.[12]

It is for this reason, I intend to argue, that ethnography has been conceived of as an instrument for data gathering and theory testing and development. This instrumentalist view distracts from a more fundamental reflection on how, and whether at all, it is possible to build peace in the current late modern capitalist global order in the first place; and on how the peace prero-gative of 'peace science' may render it complicit in the instantiation of nega-tive and imperial forms of peace.[13] As I will show, the 'writing culture' and 'Third World feminism' debates, which led to a fundamental revision of the anthropological discipline, offer crucial insights into the limits and contradic-tions of social science and its potential to effect positive social change, as well as possible strategies to better represent and support the struggles of research subjects. This discussion does not offer any final solution to the contradictions faced by peace and conflict studies, but shows how a collaborative approach to ethnographic peace research can reflect on and overcome these dilemmas by forging a dialogue *with* people affected by conflict rather than producing knowledge *on* them for Western audiences and policy actors. The article draws on debates on methodology and positionality in IR[14] and previous arguments for a more a collaborative, dialogical and 'action' or 'activist research' approach to peace and conflict research[15] to demonstrate the advan-tages of the latter vis-à-vis the currently prevailing empiricist positivism.

---

[8]Mac Ginty, *International Peacebuilding*; Richmond, *Post-Liberal Peace*.
[9]See Richmond and Mitchell, *Hybrid Forms of Peace*.
[10]See, for instance, Paffenholz, "Unpacking."
[11]See Chap. 6–9 and 15 in Richmond and Mitchell, *Hybrid Forms of Peace*.
[12]Visoka, *Peace Figuration*, 19.
[13]Jutila et al., "Resuscitating a Discipline"; Denskus, "Peacebuilding"; Turner and Kuhn, *Tyranny of Peace*.
[14]Vrasti, "Strange Case"; "Dr Strangelove"; Rancatore, "A Reply," Millenium, "Forum."
[15]Jutila et al. "Resuscitating a Discipline," 635; Millar, *Ethnographic Approach*, 133; Sabaratnam, "Avatars of Eurocentrism."

In the next section, I will review the 'local turn' literature in peace and conflict studies to argue that the 'anthropological imagination' prevailing in the field reflects the empiricist-positivist epistemology and universalist ontology prevalent in IR and political science. Subsequently, I will show how dialogical, collaborative and 'activist' research strategies developed in response to the 'writing culture' and 'Third World feminism' debates can enable scholars to overcome the essentialisms and blind spots of such 'peace science'. In the second, empirical part, I will first demonstrate how the same empiricism-positivism is mirrored in intellectual debates, social discourses and practices of peacebuilding in Kyrgyzstan. Thus, peacebuilding based on imaginaries of multiculturalism, tolerance and a 'culture of peace' are used to stabilize a socio-political equilibrium characterized by exclusion, marginalization and (structural) violence. In the final section, I will show how I avoided reproducing such imaginaries by focusing on how community security practitioners make sense of and normalize this environment, construing conflict transformation as beyond their sphere of influence.

Reception and conceptualization of ethnography in peace and conflict studies

The 'turn towards anthropology and culture'[16] in critical peacebuilding literature occurred during the gradual establishment of the critique of the 'liberal peace' and corresponding research agendas on 'hybrid' and 'post-liberal forms of peace'.[17] The new interest in 'bottom-up' and 'local agency' required new approaches and methodologies for a field largely embedded in the scientific discourse of IR and political science. Roger Mac Ginty, for instance, indicated that an 'anthropological sensitivity' was needed to study the 'bottom-up' dynamics of peacebuilding[18] and that 'some varieties of anthropology and sociology are well placed to capture these dynamics'.[19] Oliver Richmond argued that 'ethnographic methodology' could enable 'an understanding of the local, locality, context and their interactions with and against the liberal peacebuilding architecture'.[20] It appeared as if ethnographic methods would, in Vrasti's words, 'promise a type of knowledge ... more empirically accurate than that provided by discursive theories of the political'.[21]

Gearoid Millar's *An Ethnographic Approach to Peacebuilding* is the so far most comprehensive work in this intellectual synthesis. The ethnographic approach, Millar argues, 'demands a willingness to study closely the local

---

[16]Finlay, "Liberal Intervention," 226.
[17]Richmond and Mac Ginty, "Where Now?".
[18]Mac Ginty, "Indigenous Peace-Making," 139.
[19]Mac Ginty, *International Peacebuilding*, 4.
[20]Richmond, *Post-Liberal Peace*, 14, see also 75, 146, 199 ff.
[21]Vrasti, "Strange Case," 295.

social and cultural context' and 'understand how international projects are experienced by people on the ground'.[22] The added value of this approach vis-à-vis the quantitative and macro-level analyses dominating peace and conflict studies rests on 'ethnographic preparation' (meaning a thorough study of the context) and on the appraisal of cultural differences between the understandings and worldviews held by researchers and the researched, respectively.[23] The challenge to 'fully capture the local experiences of [peacebuilding] projects'[24] is framed as methodological question: 'there are dynamics within societies that demand purposeful sampling within a population if "local engagement" is to be achieved'.[25] According to this reasoning, the contextual picture of society drawn by the researcher can be approximated to the 'real' empirical situation so that data gathering and analysis enable the best possible understanding of the effects (and shortcomings) of peacebuilding interventions.

The book thus presents an instrumentalist understanding of the role of ethnography in studying post-conflict transitions and is primarily geared towards fitting the gathered data into previously established theoretical frameworks. For instance, the finding that mostly local elites benefited from the analysed projects[26] is crucial and well supported with evidence. But the constrained space given to the analysis does not allow the thorough engagement with contextual complexity and life stories of the beneficiaries as it might be expected from ethnographic research, and which might shed light on the coercive and usurping logics justifying the elite bias of projects.[27] Such streamlining is understandable as the circumstances and life cycles of peacebuilding research projects do not usually allow for long-term engagement and in-depth discussion of research findings. But the limiting effects of this should not be underestimated.

Furthermore, the instrumentalist logic underlying this ethnographic approach is illustrated by the suggestion that comprehensive analysis of the context and its complexity are not necessarily required: '[A]n ethnographic approach should not be seen as an extension of anthropology but as a tool for any discipline ... even non-anthropologists unwilling or unable to commit to this mode of ethnography can adopt and benefit from [it].'[28] This selective ethnographic approach might be effective for engaging multiple audiences. But in light of the different ways in which anthropological research has been utilized by states, militaries and the peacebuilding industry,[29] it is

[22]Millar, *Ethnographic Approach*, 3, 2.
[23]Ibid., Chap. 4 and 6.
[24]Ibid., 81.
[25]Ibid., 83.
[26]Ibid., 94–5.
[27]For a more detailed discussion see Lottholz, "Boundaries of Knowledge."
[28]Millar, *Ethnographic Approach*, 6.
[29]Finlay, "Liberal Intervention."

worth re-engaging the debate at the point where ethnography is offered as a tool to be applied at one's convenience. What does the 'healthy anthropological imagination' necessary for adopting this approach look like?[30] The understanding implicit in *An Ethnographic Approach* and the debates leading up to it implies an empiricist positivism for which anthropological research had been criticized on various occasions in the discipline's controversial legacy.[31] In this empiricist-positivist imagination, ethnography is conceived of as a tool for gathering data to confirm or refine theories, and to make peacebuilding practices more effective. This suggests that developing better peacebuilding theories and practices is a question of having the right data and methodologies. However, Denskus has argued that a focus on developing the right instruments and analysing the effectiveness of peacebuilding in delivering its alleged goals forecloses discussion about how peacebuilding is embedded in, extends and re-produces a global web of power relations.[32] In this sense, to be more effective in bringing about sustainable peace, and realistic about the possibility of doing so in the first place, peace and conflict studies would have to reflect more on its positionality within a Western-dominated international system.

Contrary to such a critical and self-reflexive stance, peace and conflict researchers' relative disinterest in the complexities and dynamics of local societies mirrors a self-understanding as 'physicians of global society' who are primarily focused on the translatability of data into research frameworks and their usefulness for theory development.[33] The framing of most peace and conflict research strongly points to a preoccupation with phenomena and concepts that are generalizable and applicable on a global level. The main problematic has thus persistently been framed in terms of the relationship between the international level and actors on the one hand, and national or local ones on the other hand.[34] In the recently published *Handbook of Disciplinary and Regional Approaches to Peace* this framing is reproduced in, for instance, considerations about 'international or grassroots positionalities' and 'localized praxis' turning 'to the international for support'.[35] Empirical exploration and 'thick description' are minimized to the extent that they yield meaningful-*cum*-generalizable insights. This reflects a universalist ontology: phenomena, ideas and concepts matter only if they are useful or meaningful in a global context. Data and phenomena that do not fit into existing theories or frameworks for (re-)interpretation are simply not relevant

---

[30]Millar, *Ethnographic Approach*, 6.
[31]Vrasti, "Strange Case," 297; Hale, "Activist Research"; Restrepo and Escobar, "World Anthropologies."
[32]Denskus, "Peacebuilding."
[33]Jutila et al., "Resuscitating a Discipline," 623.
[34]Mac Ginty, *International Peacebuilding*; Richmond, *Post-Liberal Peace*. For further critiques see Paffenholz, "Unpacking," and Graef, *Post-Liberal Peacebuilding*, Chap. 1. Mac Ginty and Richmond, discuss the critiques in "Where Now?".
[35]Richmond et al., "Introduction," 3, 4; see also 6, 8, 14 and a more nuanced discussion on pp.13–5.

enough and left behind to be studied by other disciplines. It is the exhaustion of the data available to the inquiry with this outlook that has led critical peace-building studies to turn to 'the local'.[36] Such an approach cannot but envisage ethnography as a data generation tool.

This universalist ontology and the empiricist-positivist epistemology discussed above can be traced back to the inception of peace and conflict studies.[37] One case in point is the work of John Burton, one of the co-founders of the field. He argued that the primary task of inquiry was to study and formulate the rules by which it was possible to explain conflicts with the existence of 'a generic human nature, characterized by nine ontological and probably genetic human needs'.[38] More recent contributions to 'human nature' theories of peace and conflict[39] indicate the appeal of nomological-deductive positivism and the corresponding understanding of anthropology. Arguments that anthropology 'can remind the West of the diversity of successful approaches to creating and maintaining peace'[40] continue to situate that discipline in the 'savage slot' within the intellectual division of labour of the modern episteme as it came about during the Enlightenment.[41] Anthropology is thus construed as a '[form] of knowledge that present[s] the West with its own limits by confronting it with difference and the unconscious' and 'nevertheless find[s] in Western ratio – and, hence, in European dominance – [its] reason for being'.[42]

The scientistic consensus in peace and conflict studies is not limited to the understanding of the role of ethnography and anthropology. Jutila and colleagues have argued that the field has centred around the business of a normal science – i.e. hypothesis and theory testing at the expense of critical reflection on the foundations and context of disciplinary knowledge production and a more thorough understanding of the lives of people affected by conflict.[43] A focus on open forms of violence and narrow definitions of peace has further distracted researchers from inquiring more covert forms of violence and Western countries' – and thus indirectly researchers' own – complicity with them.[44] Therefore, it was argued, a critical approach to peace and conflict research should be more self-reflexive and explicit about its limitations and political dependencies and, in methodological terms, not do research *on* conflict-affected societies, but *in dialogue with them.*[45]

---

[36]Chandler, "Peacebuilding," 25 ff.
[37]Avruch, *Culture and Conflict Resolution.*
[38]Black and Avruch, "Anthropologists in Conflictland," 34; see Burton, *Deep-Rooted Conflict.*
[39]For instance, Pinker, *Better Angels;* Fry, *Human Potential.*
[40]Souillac and Fry, "Anthropology," 75.
[41]Restrepo and Escobar, "World Anthropologies," 111;
[42]Ibid.; Richmond notices this 'fork in the path' but does not provide a solution or positioning on it; Richmond, "New Approaches," 697–8.
[43]Jutila et al., "Resuscitating a Discipline," 629.
[44]Gleditsch et al., "Peace Research," 145.
[45]Jutila et al., "Resuscitating a Discipline," 636.

Such a self-critical stance as it has been formulated from a decolonial per-spective[46] would help to highlight the link between universalist ontology/ empiricist positivism and a Western-/Eurocentric understanding of the world underlying anthropological imagination in peace and conflict studies, according to which ethnographic exploration of the periphery can help to solve problems of peace- and statebuilding.[47] This implicit cognitive mapping depoliticizes and dehistoricizes the way in which the 'periphery' or the 'Global South' has been created through imperial expansion and colo-nialism in the first place, as well as the perpetuation of this Orientalist logic, which obscures how the 'local' is 'always already' global.[48] Critical ethno-graphic peace research would inquire how categories such as 'local' or 'indi-genous' are produced, normalized and used to justify orientalizing and racializing social hierarchies.[49] The dominant consensus in peace and conflict studies, however, keeps presenting the main task of the field as the develop-ment of theories for determining and testing the preconditions for lasting peace, while reflections on the conditions of knowledge production and com-plicity with Western imperial agendas are largely avoided. As I will show in the next section, debates in anthropology have raised these criticisms towards ethnographic inquiry and helped to develop new strategies to over-come the essentialism and Eurocentrism inherent in the classical 'social science' episteme.

To embrace uncertainty: lessons from the 'Writing culture' and 'Third world feminism' debates

The empiricist anthropological imagination in peace and conflict studies bears testimony to the relative isolation in which the 'local turn' and 'post-liberal' or 'hybrid forms of peace' were theorized. Writing on the analogous 'ethnographic turn' in IR, Wanda Vrasti noted how, '[d]isre-garding the historical controversies and political aporias of ethnographic knowledge has been a necessary condition for such a "turn" to occur in the first place'.[50] The 'writing culture' and 'Third World feminism' debates had already pulled into doubt and partly done away with ideas about ethnography that have flattered peace and conflict scholars in recent years. The main lesson to be drawn from these debates is that, rather than accepting abstract and potentially problematic categories and assumptions, inquiry should focus on the very effects of categories, assumptions and ideas about how the world works. This implies a re-negotiation

---

[46]Sabaratnam, "IR in Dialogue"; "Avatars of Eurocentrism."
[47]Sabaratnam, "Avatars of Eurocentrism."
[48]Chandler, "Peacebuilding," 25; Said, "Representing the Colonized."
[49]Finlay, "Liberal Intervention," 226.
[50]Vrasti, "Strange Case," 295.

and transgression of the traditional boundaries between scholarship, practice and activism.

The 'writing culture' debate has most clearly been sparked by the volume with the same title published by James Clifford and George Marcus in 1986, alongside Marcus and Fisher's *Anthropology as Cultural Critique* (1986) and Clifford's *The Predicament of Culture* (1988).[51] Most importantly, what was at stake in this debate was the very idea of ethnography as the method for describing and trying to understand cultures: Was it really possible to write about cultures so as to describe their existence, everyday life and political struggles in a pure, objective and detached manner? Or did the act of 'writing cultures' – of describing them in words, languages and genres unknown to them – not amount to an act of construction rendering the very concept of 'culture' deeply problematic? Especially in light of the post-modern problematic faced by the social sciences, the unavoidably incomplete and necessarily distorted insight afforded by ethnography was emphasized against the background of the polyphonic, dialogical and historical nature of any cultural phenomenon.[52] One conclusion for cultural anthropology was not to downplay the inherent problems and limited possibilities of repre-senting cultures appropriately, but rather, in Vrasti's words, to 'accept … [these] disciplinary uncertainties, as something that is here to stay for anthro-pologists to work with, not as a momentary obstacle to be overcome'.[53]

Besides a 'commitment to radical perspectivism and essential reflexivity'[54] implied by this admission, another lesson was to be learned, yet. Various com-mentators observed how the 'writing culture' conversation, much like the debate in critical peacebuilding studies discussed above, revolved around the problematic of representation and giving a voice to the subaltern without reflecting on the more fundamental underpinnings of knowledge pro-duction and its embeddedness in power relations. 'Cultural critique' was for-mulated as a problem of methodology and, implicitly, of objectivity. The main goal was to somehow rid fieldwork of distorting power relations, for instance by reducing communal contact and immersion and spreading engagement over multiple locations in what Clifford termed 'multi-sited ethnography'.[55] Still, the more fundamental critique expressed during the debate on anthro-pology's 'colonial encounter' was left unaddressed by this selective self-renewal. [56] Why was it that the 'writing culture' debate took place mostly

---

[51]The insights discussed are necessarily based on a cursory reading and on reflections provided by other authors. See Restrepo and Escobar, "World Anthropologies"; Abu-Lughod, "Writing Against Culture"; Hale, "Activist Research"; Vrasti, "Strange Case."; Marcus and Fischer, *Anthropology as Cultural Critique*; and Clifford, *The Predicament of Culture*.
[52]Marcus and Fischer, *Anthropology as Cultural Critique*, Chap. 1.
[53]Vrasti, "Strange Case," 296.
[54]Ibid.
[55]Clifford, *Ethnography through Thick and Thin*.
[56]Said, "Representing the Colonized," 208; Restrepo and Escobar, "World Anthropologies," 107.

among Western or Western-affiliated scholars? What was the role of Third World anthropologists in representing culture and supporting political struggles of subaltern communities? It seemed as if anthropology would remain an inherently Eurocentric discipline with the purpose of producing knowledge on the non-West.

It is here where the 'Third World feminism' debate confronted feminism, but also anthropology, with an even more fundamental challenge.[57] In their 1984 seminal article 'Challenging Imperial Feminism', Valery Amos and Pratibha Parmar argued that 'white, mainstream feminist theory does not speak to the experiences of Black women and where it attempts to do so it is often from a racist perspective and reasoning'.[58] They found that the feminist movement was mostly concerned with the 'improvement in the material situation of a small number of white middle-class women'. 'This unconscious consensus', they posited, 'has been successful in excluding large numbers of Black women from participating in any meaningful way'.[59] The most blatant of the number of misconceptions exposed by Amos and Parmar was the argument of neo-Marxist feminists that, given the relatively better position women had attained in advanced capitalist societies, 'the changes brought by imperialism to Third World societies may, in some circumstances, have been historically progressive'.[60]

These and other interventions[61] caused a series of stand-offs; for example, the departure from the editorial board/activist collective of *Feminist Review* of the three women of colour Avtar Brah, Gail Lewis and Kum-Kum Bhavnani. In the journal's 25th anniversary issue, the protagonists explain: 'We said we would come back if [the other editors] make a sincere commitment that "race" is not something that not only we bring up, it's something to do with all of us and everybody has to own it.'[62] The journal collective eventually decided to take on this responsibility:

> *Feminist Review* wants to challenge the racist discourses that increasingly pervade our globalized world. ... We want to continue the work analysing and confronting racist representations of women, and the deepening and entrenched intersections of race, gender, class and sexuality.[63]

This episode proved that, '[w]ith its conflictual histories ... feminism cannot ever denote fully a set of unified, essential or self-evident practices either in the

---

[57]Cf. Abu-Lughod, "Writing Against Culture" for an integrated discussion of cultural and feminist critique. I omit the concurrently used term 'Women of Colour Feminism' for sake of brevity.
[58]Amos and Parmar, "Challenging Imperial Feminism," 45.
[59]Ibid.
[60]Maxine Molyneux cited in ibid., 48.
[61]Moraga and Anzaldúa, *This Bridge Called My Back*; Mohanty, "Under Western Eyes," Minh-Ha, "Difference."
[62]Avtar Brah in Brah et al., "A Feminist Review Roundtable," 202.
[63]"Editorial," 5.

West, in the postcolonial world, or in the encounter between them'.[64] Rather, it would be a diverse movement requiring constant dialogue and exchange. The *Feminist review* itself tried to address this by establishing the involvement of international 'corresponding editors' from different non-Western settings and by giving a platform for women from various places to tell their own stories of their struggles.[65]

The main lesson to be drawn from this debate is that knowledge production cannot be emancipatory regardless of who is doing it or by virtue of its 'radical' or 'emancipatory' outlook. Rather, in order to describe and engage with political struggles, it is indispensable to involve people in a debate to establish a commonly shared picture of the problem and ideas for possible solutions. If reality is indeed non-unitary and always dialogical, polyphonic and controversial, then academic inquiry should make an effort to reflect this complexity and not try to condense it. In this sense, collaborative knowledge production is not a quick fix for social scientists to once again produce a 'better' account of 'reality'. It rather implies to let go of the empiricist imagination that there is one 'reality', which can have an accurate reflection that foregrounds possible action. In this sense, embracing uncertainty,[66] anti-essentialism and 'radical perspectivism' also comes at a price, as questions as to how and by whom oppression is produced – and what constitutes oppression in the first place – take primacy over a more targeted and unified struggle.

But the two debates have also helped to develop more action-oriented strategies. The collaborative, dialogical approach to knowledge production practiced in the *Feminist Review*, which tries to engage dialogically with the struggles of people rather than merely documenting and translating them into the Western academic episteme, foregrounded concrete actions which were more appropriate than those devised by the older, more Western-centric scholarship. The underlying idea of transcending the confines of standard academic research to support the political struggle of groups subject to research is key to an 'activist research' paradigm.[67] Such an approach is focused on experiences, knowledge and opinions that do not correspond to Western academic standards of what constitutes relevant knowledge and of distance and impartiality.[68] Similarly, recent discussions on practice theory in IR and social science[69] have indicated how following actors in their daily conduct and engaging with them *on their terms* can enable a critical analysis of how certain types of knowledge, expertise and practices – such as peace-

---

[64]Spurlin, "resisting heteronormativity," 13.
[65]See, for instance, the two editorials by Teacher and Shukrallah and by Azim, reprinted in the 25th anniversary issue of *Feminist Review*.
[66]Denskus, "Peacebuilding," 661.
[67]Hale, "Activist Research"; "Introduction".
[68]Hale, "Activist Research," 101.
[69]For instance, Büger and Gadinger, *International Practice Theory*; Kustermans, "Practice Turn."

and statebuilding – are embedded in and reproduce global power relations.[70] As I will show in section four, the challenges of a dialogical and collaborative approach are offset by the insights enabled through such long-term engagement and knowledge production that refrains from imposing 'home-made theoretical puzzles' on its subjects.[71]

The deceptive power of emancipatory ideas: multiculturalism, tolerance and the 'Culture of peace' in Kyrgyzstan

The aim of the second part of the article is to illustrate the theoretical argument through a discussion of the dilemmas of peacebuilding in the Kyrgyz Republic in Central Asia. The empiricist positivism, universalist ontology and prioritization of theory building and testing over thick contextual description, which I critiqued above, is apparent in domestic and international peace and conflict scholarship on this country. Such scholarship and corresponding peacebuilding policies, with their focus on the promotion of diversity, tolerance and a 'culture of peace', forego the chance to discuss significant root causes and factors of conflict, as well as everyday experiences of injustice and exclusion. In such an environment, where peacebuilding and interethnic reconciliation have become the prime imperatives and dominant narratives, researchers cannot rely on ethnographic data gathering for capturing the dynamics of post-conflict transition. To overcome this impasse, critical ethnographic peace research should extend existing analyses of how imaginaries and discourses of 'culture', 'tolerance' and 'peace' can conceal or even (re-) produce trajectories of 'authoritarian conflict management' that provide little space for disagreement and raising questions of justice and equality.[72]

The trajectories of the five Central Asian republics following their independence from the Soviet Union in 1991 have differed considerably, with Turkmenistan and Uzbekistan establishing and entrenching authoritarian governance and Tajikistan, Kazakhstan and Kyrgyzstan introducing different forms and degrees of reform and liberalization.[73] Kyrgyzstan embraced the liberal-democratic reform blue print most comprehensively and was promoted as 'island of democracy' by its first post-independence president Askar Akayev.[74] Economic shock therapy and trade liberalization did not bring prosperity or development, however, but plunged large parts of the population into severe poverty, leading to political instability and two revolutions in 2005 and 2010. In June 2010, a series of smaller clashes spiralled into

---

[70]Graef, *Post-Liberal Peacebuilding*, ch. 3; Paffenholz, "Unpacking," 868.
[71]Vrasti, "Strange Case," 286.
[72]Lewis, "Central Asia."
[73]See ibid. for a more detailed discussion.
[74]Marat, "Imagined Past."

violent confrontations in and around the cities of Osh and Jalal-Abad in southern Kyrgyzstan, causing almost 500 deaths and the displacement of hundreds of thousands.[75] The 'Osh' or 'June events' – framed as interethnic conflict between Kyrgyz and Uzbeks, the country's second-largest population group, in the international and much of the national media[76] – attracted much international attention and large-scale peacebuilding, post-conflict reconstruction and conflict prevention programmes from the Organization for Co-Operation and Security in Europe (OSCE), the UN and international NGOs.

Kyrgyzstan thus became another 'Peaceland' and instructive research site for peace and conflict scholars. An ever-growing network of national implementing partners worked to promote peaceful coexistence, interethnic tolerance and prevention of further conflict.[77] This interest in peacebuilding was not new: already in the 1990s, various centres and academic departments for conflict resolution, conflict prevention and 'conflictology' had constituted a sizeable part of intellectual life.[78] Noteworthy is the UNESCO-funded Centre for Conflict Prevention's creation of the journal *Central Asia and the Culture of Peace*, whose task it was to 'unite the efforts of local and international intellectuals to develop a conception of a culture of peace, … [analyse] the multifarious aspects of tolerance, and promote ideas and principles of dialogue between cultures and religions'.[79] According to a 2005 editorial, the journal was to host a process in which 'politicians, scholars, and societal actors of many countries realize[d] the development and promotion of ideas and conceptions of peacebuilding … in the 21st century'.[80] Peacebuilding, conflict prevention, and tolerance were formulated as a matter of the Kyrgyzstani people bethinking the virtues inherent in its civilizational heritage and thereby mastering the challenges of integration into a globalized world.[81] The task of the intellectual community was to formulate theories and concepts for the realization and stabilization of peace on the national and international levels, rather than researching the reasons and mechanisms leading to different forms of violence. The Kyrgyzstani version of 'peace science' was born and spawned the concepts that would shape peacebuilding for the years to come.

The peacebuilding and promotion of tolerance in post-2010 Kyrgyzstan is a continuation of the civilizational 'culture of peace' discourse and the problem-solving, empiricist-positivist peace epistemology underlying it.

---

[75] Estimates revolve around 470 deaths, 400,000 internally displaced persons and 110,000 who (temporarily) left the country. See Matveeva et al., "Tragedy," and the report of the independent but contested Kyrgyzstan Inquiry Commission under http://www.kgzembind.in/Report%20(English).pdf.

[76] This framing was heavily contested by the government, though; see Megoran et al., "Peacebuilding and Reconciliation Projects."

[77] Ibid.

[78] Reeves, "Locating Danger."

[79] The announcement can be found at http://www.kyrnatcom.unesco.kz/conflict%20centre.htm. All translations from Russian are the author's.

[80] Toktosunova, "From the Editor," 5.

[81] Ibid.

A guide titled *Building Peace and Interethnic Harmony in Kyrgzystan*, for instance, argues that 'every person can do something for the formation of a culture of peace, mutual respect and understanding within society' while sources of conflict are rooted in 'impatience, stereotypes, and misconceptions about people of other cultures and ethnic belonging'.[82] Another example is a methods guide for schoolteachers titled *The formation of tolerance (Pedagogy of peace)*, which 'is devised for the formation of tolerant behaviour among the young generation' and 'give[s] an opportunity to young people to acquire knowledge and skills necessary for the prevention of violence and for the peaceful solution of conflicts'.[83] The prevention and solution of conflict is thus framed as a question of knowledge, skills, and the unlocking of people's potential for peace. Such a problem-solving 'peace focus' risks disregarding sources and occurrences of conflict and intolerance, such as inequality and identity-based discrimination. Critical analyses of the latter provide an alternative view but are given little attention given the government's and also donors' attempts to emphasize positive potentials and results.[84]

A priority of peacebuilding and conflict prevention projects was to reach out to the communities that had been directly affected by the 'Osh events'. For instance, a project on 'peace messengers' (Russian: *vestniki mira*; Kyrgyz: *yntymak zharchylary*) was jointly carried out by the OSCE, local NGOs and authorities and recruited over 300 volunteers from across the entire south of Kyrgyzstan. A 2013 report states that this institution 'demonstrated particular skills in the peaceful solution of conflict situations, in countering rumours and provocations, [and] participation in the regulation of emergency situations'.[85] 'Peace messengers' are presented as 'the logical extension of traditional institutions of popular democracy' – as their teams are made up of 'civil society, religious leaders [imams], traditional leaders such as elder courts [*aksakals*, lit. "white beard"], businessmen and ordinary members of a given community'[86] with 'contemporary methodologies for the resolution of conflict situations at their disposal'.[87] Through mandatory 'common values', the project promoted a uniting vision including tolerance and patriotism, which was defined as 'devotion to and love for one's Fatherland, one's people ... [and] *not to be confused with nationalism or chauvinism*'.[88] With its rootedness in local communities and their traditions and interests, this project presents a case of hybrid and post-liberal forms of peace and lends itself to ethnographic inquiry. However, both this and other peace- and tolerance-promoting projects are insufficient in tackling

---

[82]Alisheva, *Building Peace*, 6–7.
[83]Shamudinova, *Formation of Tolerance*, 7.
[84]Megoran et al., "Peacebuilding and Reconciliation Projects'"; Reeves, "Locating Danger."
[85]Anonymous, *Peace Messengers*, 5.
[86]Ibid., 9.
[87]Ibid., 5.
[88]Ibid., 12; emphasis added.

the precarious living conditions in the conflict-affected communities and the covert everyday forms of discrimination.[89] Correspondingly, rather than focus on the everyday forms of peace and their utilization or promotion in peacebuilding practices, ethnographic research should focus on everyday forms of conflict, which, in their hidden way, are often more present in and impeding on people's lives.

The peace messengers' mission statement highlights the rationale of uniting people under the banner of a civic, multicultural nationalism, as it was promoted by the slogans 'Kyrgyzstan – Our common home' since 1991 and 'peoples' friendship' (druzhba narodov) during the Soviet era.[90] Multicultural or civic nationalism is the underlying rationale of many peacebuilding concepts, practices and projects in Kyrgyzstan.[91] This approach is reasonable given that adults were brought up with ideals of multicultural diversity and tolerance under the above-mentioned banners and can thus easily identify with this message.[92] Still, diversity, tolerance and 'people's friendship' are also deeply problematic in the context of the historical and ongoing patterns of identitarian policy-making that pit the poorer parts of identity communities against each other and let such peacebuilding slogans ring empty. The most infamous purpose of the 'peoples' friendship' ideal was to soothe the sense of loss emanating from the Soviet 'divide and rule' policy, by which the five Soviet Republics in Central Asia had been created in such a way that some communities were cut off from their 'home' national republics.[93] The privileging of the majority or 'titular' ethnicities in their respective republics – e.g. granting them access to administrative and political offices and careers – led to a slow but steady marginalization of minorities, forcing them to retreat into non-public sector professions.[94] Especially when the Soviet economic model came under increasing strain in the 1980s and more people from rural Kyrgyzstan migrated to urban centres, tensions in the competition for jobs, housing and land intensified and erupted into deadly clashes in and around Osh in the year 1990 which.[95] After independence, the marginalization of Uzbeks and other minorities intensified due to the increasingly precarious economic situation and the perception that Uzbeks, traditionally more successful in trade and business, were generally better off than Kyrgyz.[96] Different authors have argued that the 2010

---

[89]Bennett, "Everything."

[90]Marat, "Imagined Past," 15; Gaziyev, Ethnonationalism. This was confirmed by follow-up research on the project conducted in July 2012 and in July 2015.

[91]See activities of one of the largest national NGOs, the Foundation for Tolerance International (http://www.fti.org.kg/en/about-us/our-work) and priority areas of the UN Peacebuilding Fund (http://www.unpbf.org/countries/kyrgyzstan/).

[92]Marat, "Imagined Past."

[93]Ibid.; Gaziyev, Ethnonationalism.

[94]Ibid.; Ismailbekova and Karimova, "Conflict Dynamics."

[95]Tishkov, "Don't Kill Me."

[96]Ibid.; Megoran et al., "Peacebuilding and Reconciliation Projects."

clashes, which disproportionately led to the destruction of Uzbek properties, businesses and loss of Uzbek lives, happened against a background of rising ethno-nationalist sentiments and calls for a re-assertion of Kyrgyz sovereignty vis-à-vis minorities.[97]

The 'peoples' friendship' thus turned out to be as ambiguous and dependent on growth and prosperity as ideas of multiculturalism and diversity in other contexts. For those believing in the 'peoples' friendship' and a tolerant, multicultural Kyrgyzstan, the Osh events were a rude awakening. In both the Kyrgyz and the Uzbek communities, many people had not held any grievances against the other group, helped each other during the conflict and did all they could to reconcile people. The corresponding cognitive dissonance is best expressed in one example of a peacebuilding event described by Megoran and others, where a Kyrgyz head teacher pledged that interethnic friendship 'may never be broken' and 'it will be as if nothing happened'.[98] This kind of denial is remarkable but appears to represent a narrative that many are clinging to.[99] Especially elite and educated strata of society tend to accept or downplay the ethnicity-based grievances and fail to acknowledge the actual level of alienation and hardship experienced by many. Issues of political representation and post-conflict justice remain unmentioned for fear of confrontation and reprisal by authorities.[100] People facing discrimination and harassment have to raise these issues anonymously,[101] or, as in the case of Kyrgyzstani Uzbeks, develop coping strategies such as moving into Uzbek majority neighbourhoods and avoiding certain parts of the city.[102]

What contribution can ethnographic peace research make in such a situation, where voices and events departing from the ideal picture of 'culture of peace', tolerance and multicultural diversity are silenced, downplayed or outright denied out of a longing for peace? Research and practices based on such a viewpoint are likely to produce practices of mere conflict management instead of initiating more fundamental discussions of inequality, injustices and marginalization. While their contributions are important, the emphasis that most peacebuilding projects put on the mediation of disagreements and peaceful resolution of antagonisms renders the discussion and addressing of socio-economic inequality and experiences of harassment and exclusion, a secondary issue or affords it no space at all. A simple focus on 'peacebuilding' and 'everyday forms of peace' thus risks unawareness about the continuous reproduction of conflict and its root causes. As these problems are often

---

[97]Ibid.; Matveeva et al., "Tragedy."
[98]Megoran et al., "Peacebuilding and Reconciliation Projects," 16.
[99]On several occasions during my fieldwork middle-aged Kyrgyz interviewees shared their visions of society based on multiculturalist idea and their wish that 'everything was as it used to be' (26 June, Bishkek; 9 November, Bishkek).
[100]Lottholz, "Negative Post-Liberal Peace."
[101]See Bennett, "Everything."
[102]Ismailbekova and Karimova, "Conflict Dynamics."

invisible or hard to uncover, especially for foreign researchers who are often denied access and participation,[103] adopting an ethnographic approach would not help to yield the critical insights I have provided by looking at the existing research. I will show how this critical picture can foreground the application of ethnographic methods for a strategy of collaborative research on the dilemma situations faced by peace and security practitioners.

Collaborative research: new insights into community security practices and governmentality

As argued in section two, getting better insights into peoples' everyday lives and political struggles is not only a question of methodology, but can be best achieved with a collaborative approach at doing research. This means that the prevalent conception of fieldwork as a one-off data gathering – if not *extraction* – exercise preceding analysis needs to be rethought as a long-term and dialogical process. To fully take into account the way in which the worldviews of different protagonists affect the conduct and outcomes of peacebuilding projects, arranging a long-term conversation between researcher and relevant organizations or communities appears the most promising way. It offers the possibility of understanding how the very categories and theories used in peace and conflict studies themselves produce unintended side effects of hierarchy, differentiation and exclusion.[104] Ethnography can thus help, in Finlay's words, 'to understand how so-called communal identities and indigenous practices are produced, subsumed and reproduced in peacebuilding, i.e. how they are made useful to government'.[105] This transcends the classical Foucauldian understanding about the effects of discourse and combines it with Bourdieu's practice theory to trace how epistemic frameworks become socially acknowledged and (re-) produced.[106] Furthermore, it can be easier to gain trust and access with organizations and groups when their practices are the main research interest: This signals that they will not have to learn any new terminology introduced by the researcher and may draw insights from the researcher's analysis.[107]

Collaborative and dialogical research brings with it some challenges, however. The criteria by which researchers' success or impact is measured in academia are in many ways diametrically opposed to what partners in the world of NGOs, policy-makers and social movements expect.[108] The

---

[103]Bekmurzaev et al., "Navigating Safety Implications."
[104]Sabaratnam, "Avatars of Eurocentrism."
[105]Finlay, "Liberal Intervention," 231.
[106]Ibid.; see also Graef, *Post-Liberal Peacebuilding*, Chap. 1; Millar, *Ethnographic Approach*, 103; Rancatore, "A Reply," 74–5.
[107]Bekmurzaev et al., "Navigating Safety Implications," Graef, *Post-Liberal Peacebuilding*, Chap. 4; Millar, *Ethnographic Approach*, 140.
[108]Hale, "Activist Research," 110–1.

latter primarily need outputs that help to raise awareness and, ideally, attract financial support, meaning the respective organization or project should be presented in a positive light and in an accessible language. Academic journal articles or books do not meet these criteria on several counts, so that requests to comment and approve academic research outputs present additional labour for partners in the field, with no near-term benefits in sight. Disagreement and disappointments over presentation and scope of analysis can prove to be a major challenge.[109] In my own collaborative research with the Kyrgyzstani NGO network 'Civic Union "For Reforms and Result"' (CURR; Russian: *Grazhdanskiy Soyuz 'Za reformy i rezultat'*), whose members I accompanied to meetings and trainings in different partner communities across the country, I tried to take these needs into account. By publishing initial research insights in genres more familiar and accessible to this organization and its potential supporters,[110] I showcased how my research could shed light on the positive change effected by their promotion of new approaches to community security provision and cooperation between law enforcement, local authorities and the population.[111]

The research I was able to carry out in accompanying this organization in its efforts to implement community security projects in different localities yielded multiple insights into the problems faced by local community security working groups, as well as the pressure they felt to take measures against perceived security threats.[112] The working group of one town in south-western Kyrgyzstan,[113] for instance, felt helpless in trying to curb the activity of foreign missionaries which was allegedly causing increasing (religious) radicalization of the local population, with young people reportedly going to join the fighting in Syria.[114] This made one group member posit that it might be best to 'completely prohibit' such missionary activities. But the deputy head of the local administration urged more modesty and compliance with the law: 'Our main goal is to maintain public control. I agree [the foreign missionaries need to be controlled] but it has to be according to some rules [*na baze kakikh-to pravil*].' The ensuing discussion also tackled the issue of the young generation's apathy and lack of direction given high rates of unemployment and a profoundly inadequate educational system. The senior neighbourhood inspector of the police provoked an outcry among the group with his proposal that the state should conscript a higher number of young men for military

---

[109]See Mosse, "Anti-Social Anthropology?", 946 ff.

[110]For instance, Lottholz, "Polizeireform"; Lottholz, "Police Reform."

[111]To the extent that this research was 'predicated on alignment with a group organized in struggle, and on collaborative relations of knowledge productions with members of that group', it could also be called activist research according to Hale's definition ("Introduction," 20).

[112]Cf. Lottholz, "Police Reform."

[113]All following quotes translated from Russian or Kyrgyz and taken from a participatory observation during a planning event on 11 November 2015 if not indicated otherwise.

[114]CURR, "Security Together."

service to enhance their 'discipline'. This was opposed most outspokenly for the Kyrgyz nationalist undertone such a policy would imply. The group leader explained her view of the underlying problem:

> You know what the problem is all about? We don't have any men, there are only women in the schools ... Racketeering is spreading without any male authorities fighting it ... in any case, a man is a man [*vse ravno, muzhchina – eto muzhchina*].

Although misogynist at first sight, this is a legitimate description of the reality in today's Kyrgyzstan, where a significant part of the male population have to work abroad to provide for their families. Children are left behind with grandparents, extended family or even neighbours, which led to a precarious lack of authority and a rising trend in juvenile delinquency. This is paired with an often ignorant and patronizing attitude vis-à-vis youth, which was palpable on another participatory observation I conducted during a training session with a working group in a village north of Bishkek.[115] In my only interjection during the session, I asked why the group was not consulting their youngest member when discussing possibilities of keeping young people busy to prevent juvenile delinquency and 'hooliganism'. 'He sits quite far away [*daleko sidit*]', responded one attendee, and another dismissed my suggestion: 'The elderly will sort it out for him [*Dla nego pozhilye reshaiut*].' On another occasion, the working group failed to listen to the representative of so-called 'new arrivals', people settled in the village from elsewhere in the country, about whom there had been different complaints of misconduct. These two instances show how failure to communicate with vulnerable and supposedly 'problematic' groups is likely to lead to the devising and execution of measures which may disenfranchise and alienate the people concerned.

These examples illustrate how people dealing with questions of community security try to make sense of the challenges they face and devise ways to tackle them. Rather than taking them for granted, this research attempts to analyse how communal or group identities – in this case followers of 'non-traditional religion' (formulation used in place of 'radical Islam'),[116] youth and 'new arrivals' – are being constituted and used in the analysis and tackling of problems. In subsequent discussions, my interlocutors told me that they and their local partners were aware of these aspects and trying to address them.[117] In this sense, my research did not yield decisive insights for the practitioners themselves, as it merely described and contextualized the dilemmas they faced. But as I have argued above, this is exactly the contribution of collaborative and

---

[115]30 November 2015.
[116]CURR, "Security Together."
[117]Interview with representative of CURR; Bishkek/Birmingham, 26 March 2016; correspondence with representative of international NGO Saferworld, March 2016.

practice-focused research, i.e. to show how community security practitioners construe challenges and ways to tackle them with the instruments at their disposal; and to provide a critical assessment and reflection on their actions and thus potentially uncover blind spots that might otherwise go unnoticed.[118]

As regards the logics of municipality level community security and peacebuilding, fundamental changes in national legislation and policy are routinely seen as lying beyond the scope of these working groups' activities, as they require more concerted efforts on the regional and national level.[119] The analysis can thus show how exclusion, marginalization and hidden forms of conflict are merely 'managed' or even accepted to maintain often *thin* forms of 'security' and 'peace', while the task of addressing underlying inequalities and tensions in a more fundamental manner is deferred into the future and to other actors and arenas.[120] Rather than using clearly problematic categories and concepts in the pursuit of the dominant logic of theory building and testing, a critical approach to ethnographic peace research should thus show how categories and identities are produced and used in practice, and forge a dialogue with practitioners as to how the securitizing logic of mere conflict management can be challenged and overcome. Furthermore, by engaging with community security practitioners on the ground, I have shown how research can shed light on the preconditions (e.g. resource and personnel scarcity, little participation) of identity-based and essentialist security and peacebuilding practices.

Conclusion

In this article, I have argued against empiricist positivism and for a collaborative and dialogical approach towards ethnographic peace research. First, I posited that the 'anthropological imagination' in peace and conflict studies is reflecting the universalist ontology and empiricist-positivist epistemology dominating the field. Thus, the purpose of ethnography is understood as gathering data to consolidate the theoretical understanding of conflict and solutions to it in a global or macro-level perspective. I have argued that this ontology needs to be overcome and have affirmed the calls that, instead of continuing to use the categories that have dominated the inquiry so far, research should focus on the very processes of the (re-) production of governmentality through categories such as 'local' and 'international', 'bottom-up' and 'top-down', etc. In section two, I discussed how the 'writing culture' and 'Third World feminism' debates presented a major challenge to the discipline of anthropology and its conceptual apparatus, so that empiricist

---

[118]Correspondence with CURR representative, 30 March 2017.
[119]Lottholz, "Police Reform," 27.
[120]See Graef, *Post-Liberal Peacebuilding*, 51 ff.

imagination and the instrumentalist understanding of ethnography were challenged and (partly) done away with. The critical scholarship of those days found that uncertainty and controversy were to be embraced in an effort at dialogical knowledge production together *with* the communities in scope rather than *for* them. In the second part I have illustrated the theoretical argument by showing how research focusing on 'peace' and its 'local' and culturally specific forms – such as the imaginaries of a 'culture of peace' and tolerance in Kyrgyzstan – is likely to overlook trajectories of exclusion, marginalization and 'conflict management'. Ethnographic data gathering is bound to miss out on such trajectories as well, especially when done by foreign researchers and given people's fixation on peace and harmony. As I showed in the final section, research on community security practices through a collaborative and practice-based framework facilitates access to discussions on what is going on in communities and gives an insight into how the maintenance of security and peace is entangled with different methods of profiling, 'othering' and patronizing of certain groups. This analysis integrates Foucauldian discursive analysis with Bourdieusian practice theory and helps to show how practitioners adapt and reproduce epistemic frameworks and analytical categories, which have certain ordering, hierarchizing and potentially exclusionary effects.

I am aware that much of this article might be vulnerable to criticisms for the essentialisms and simplifications it tries to oppose. But my critique is not aimed at identifying any specific, explicitly empiricist approaches or a positivist 'straw man'. Rather, I tried to show how the ontological and epistemological assumptions of peace and conflict scholars – stemming from the institutionalization of the scientific field and perhaps enabling in the first place – are apparent in the way in which most research is still framed. Also, initiatives to reduce the abstractness and disconnect of academic inquiry from its potential beneficiaries already do exist.[121] But the relatively little attention they receive in comparison to the mainstream genres of academic publishing shows that the political economy of knowledge production in the field is far from shifting. Against this trend, a critical approach towards ethnographic peace research can take a step towards being more dialogical by incorporating the feedback and alternative viewpoints of those informants and interlocutors who are ready and able to respond to the way in which they and their societies are represented; and further by challenging the epistemic privilege of Western/Western-affiliated scholars and engaging scholars and practitioners from peripheral 'Peacelands' in a conversation. Instead of a data-gathering tool, ethnography could thus be made a reflexive practice which is conscious of the processes of translation and (re-) interpretation

---

[121]See, for instance, the 'Hearing Voices Project' (http://www.hearingvoicesproject.org/), or 'Pax in Nuce' magazine (https://pcdnetwork.org/blogs/pax-in-nuce-new-online-magazine/).

occurring in its course.[122] By challenging and transforming power relations structuring the current global political economy of knowledge production, a dialogical approach towards ethnographic peace research could 'give voice' to its subjects rather than 'objectify' them.

Acknowledgements

I would like to thank Nicolas Lemay-Hébert, Aksana Ismailbekova, Franco Galdini, and Karolina Kluczewska for their comments and guidance in writing this article. An earlier version was presented at the Annual Conference of the Association of Social Anthropologists of the UK and Commonwealth, Exeter, 14 April 2015, where I received much appreciated comments. I am most indebted to my collaboration partners in Kyrgyzstan, mostly Timur and Alexey, as they enabled my research and patiently engaged in follow-up discussions. Many thanks also to Gearoid Millar and two anonymous reviewers for providing crucial feedback and suggestions that helped to further develop this work. All errors remain my own.

Disclosure statement

No potential conflict of interest was reported by the author.

Funding

The work on this article was supported by the School of Government and Society, Doctoral Research Bursary and the International Development Department (both University of Birmingham), and the Centre for East European and International Studies (Berlin).

Bibliography

Abu-Lughod, Lila. "Writing Against Culture." In *Recapturing Anthropology Working in the Present*, edited by Richard G. Fox, 137–54. Santa Fe: School of American Research Press, 1991.

Alisheva, Artykul R., ed. *Postroenie mira i mezhetnicheskogo soglasia v Kyrgyzstane Posobie dlya islamskogo dukhovenstva OMSU i aktivistov mestnykh soobshestv* [Building Peace and Interethnic Harmony in Kyrgyzstan – A Guide for the

---

[122]Vrasti, "Dr Strangelove."

Islamic Clergy, Organs of Local Self-Governance and Activists of Local Communities], Supported by UN Peacebuilding Fund, 2015. http://unpbf.kg/wp-content/uploads/2015/12/merged_PosobieRUS-FINAL.pdf (accessed November 9, 2016).

Amos, Valerie, and Pratibha Parmar. "Challenging Imperial Feminism." *Feminist Review* 17 (1984): 44–63.

Anonymous. "Editorial."*Feminist Review* 40 (1992): 1–5.

Anonymous, *Yntymak Zharchylary – Vestniki Mira* [Peace Messengers; in Kyrgyz and Russian]. Bishkek: OSCE Centre in Bishkek, 2013. Unpublished document.

Autesserre, Séverine. *Peaceland: Conflict Resolution and the Everyday Politics of International Intervention.* New York: Cambridge University Press, 2014.

Avruch, Kevin. *Culture and Conflict Resolution.* Washington, DC: US Institute of Peace Press, 1998.

Bekmurzaev, Nurbek, Joshua R. Meyer and Philipp Lottholz. "Navigating the Safety Implications of Doing Research and Being Researched in Kyrgyzstan: Cooperation, Networks, Framing." *Central Asian Survey*, forthcoming.

Bennett, Will. *Everything Can Be Tolerated – Except Injustice.* Osh: Saferworld, 2016. http://www.saferworld.org.uk/resources/view-resource/1050-ldquoeverything-can-be-tolerated-ndash-except-injusticerdquo (accessed November 9, 2016).

Black, Peter W., and Kevin Avruch. "Anthropologists in Conflictland: The Role of Cultural Anthropology in an Institute for Conflict Analysis and Resolution." *Polar: Political and Legal Anthropology Review* 16, no. 3 (1993): 29–38.

Bliesemann de Guevara, Berit, ed. *Statebuilding and State-Formation: The Political Sociology of Intervention.* London: Routledge, 2012.

Brah, Avtar, et al. "A Feminist Review Roundtable on the Un/Certainties of the Routes of the Collective and the Journal." *Feminist Review* 80 (2005): 198–219.

Burton, John W. *Resolving Deep-Rooted Conflict: A Handbook.* Lanham: University Press of America, 1987.

Büger, Christian, and Frank Gadinger. *International Practice Theory: New Perspectives.* Basingstoke: Palgrave, 2014.

Chandler, David. "Peacebuilding and the Politics of Non-Linearity: Rethinking 'Hidden' Agency and 'Resistance.'" *Peacebuilding* 1, no. 1 (2013): 17–32.

Civic Union 'For Reforms and Result' [CURR]. "Bezopasnost soobsha - Itogi pro-grammy po razvitiu sotsialnogo partnerstva v podderzhanii pravoporiadka i profi-laktike pravonarushenii - finalnyi otchet" [Security Together – Results of the Programme for the Development of Social Partnership in Support of the Rule of Law and Crime Prevention – Final Report]. Bishkek: CURR, 2016. http://reforma.kg/sites/default/files/analytics/crime-prevention-report-web.pdf

Clifford, James. *The Predicament of Culture.* Cambridge: Harvard University Press, 1988.

Clifford, James. *Ethnography through Thick and Thin.* Princeton, NJ: Princeton University Press, 1998.

Denskus, Tobias. "Peacebuilding Does Not Build Peace." *Development in Practice* 17, no. 4–5 (2007): 656–62.

Distler, Werner. "Intervention as a Social Practice: Knowledge Formation and Transfer in the Everyday of Police Missions." *International Peacekeeping* 23, no. 2 (2016): 326–49.

Finlay, Andrew. "Liberal Intervention, Anthropology and the Ethnicity Machine." *Peacebuilding* 3, no. 3 (2015): 224–37.

Fry, Douglas P. *The Human Potential for Peace.* New York: Oxford University Press, 2006.

Gaziyev, Jamshid. *Ethnonationalism in Central Asia: Inter-Ethnic Conflicts and Institutionalized Ethnicity in the Land of Eternal Friendship and Brotherly Nations*. Saarbrücken: LAP Lambert, 2010.

Graef, Julian. *Practicing Post-Liberal Peacebuilding: Legal Empowerment and Emergent Hybridity in Liberia*. Baskingstoke: Palgrave, 2015.

Gleditsch, Nils Petter, Jonas Nordkvelle, and Håvard Strand. "Peace Research – Just the Study of War?" *Journal of Peace Research* 51, no. 2 (2014): 145–58.

Hale, Charles R. "Activist Research v. Cultural Critique: Indigenous Land Rights and the Contradictions of Politically Engaged Anthropology." *Cultural Anthropology* 21, no. 1 (2006): 96–120.

Hale, Charles R. "Introduction." In *Engaging Contradictions: Theory, Politics, and Methods of Activist Scholarship*, edited by Charles R. Hale, 1–28. Berkeley: University of California Press, 2008.

Ismailbekova, Aksana, and Baktygul Karimova. "Ethnic Differentiation and Conflict Dynamics: Uzbeks Marginalization and Non-Marginalization in Southern Kyrgyzstan." In *Understanding the City through its Margins: Pluridisciplinary Perspectives from Case Studies in Africa, Asia and the Middle East*, ed. André Chappatte, Ulrike Freitag, and Nora Lafi. London: Routledge, forthcoming.

Jutila, Matti, Samu Pehkonen, and Tarja Väyrynen. "Resuscitating a Discipline: An Agenda for Critical Peace Research." *Millennium* 36 no. 3 (2008): 623–40.

Kustermans, Jorg. "Parsing the Practice Turn: Practice, Practical Knowledge, Practices." *Millennium* 44, no. 2 (2016): 175–96.

Lewis, David. "Central Asia: Contested Peace." In *The Palgrave Handbook of Disciplinary and Regional Approaches to Peace*, ed. Oliver P. Richmond, Sandra Pogodda, and Jasmin Ramovic, 387–96. Basingstoke: Palgrave, 2016.

Lottholz, Philipp. "A Negative Post-Liberal Peace? Inquiring the Implications of Peacebuilding Discourses and Practices in Central Asia." In *Conflict Management After Empire in Eurasia: Beyond the Liberal Peace*, edited by Catherine Owen, Shairbek Juraev, David Lewis, Nick Megoran, John Heathershaw, and Ian Campbell. New York: Rowman & Littlefield, forthcoming.

Lottholz, Philipp. "Exploring the Boundaries of Knowledge via Hybridity." *Journal of Intervention and Statebuilding* 10, no. 1 (2016): 136–42.

Lottholz, Philipp. "Police Reform in Kyrgyzstan: Community Security Mechanisms as a Step towards Fundamental Change?" *Central Asia Policy Review* 3, no. 1 (2016): 22–27.

Lottholz, Philipp. "Polizeireform in Kirgistan: Mechanismen der Gemeindesicherheit als Schritt zum fundamentalen Wandel?" *Zentralasien-Analysen* No. 99 (2016) http://www.laender-analysen.de/zentralasien/pdf/ZentralasienAnalysen99.pdf (accessed April 10, 2016).

Mac Ginty, Roger. "Indigenous Peace-Making versus the Liberal Peace." *Cooperation and Conflict* 43, no. 2 (2008): 139–63.

Mac Ginty, Roger. *International Peacebuilding and Local Resistance: Hybrid Forms of Peace*. Basingstoke: Palgrave, 2011.

Marat, Erica. "Imagined Past, Uncertain Future: The Creation of National Ideologies in Kyrgyzstan and Tajikistan." *Problems of Post-Communism* 55, no. 1 (2008): 12–24.

Marcus, George E., and Michael M. J. Fischer. *Anthropology as Cultural Critique: An Experimental Moment in the Human Sciences*. Chicago: University of Chicago Press, 1986.

Matveeva, Anna, Savin Igor, and Bahrom Faizullaev. "Kyrgyzstan: Tragedy in the South." Ethnopolitics Paper No. 17, 2012, http://www.valerytishkov.ru/engine/documents/document1928.pdf (accessed November 9, 2016).

Megoran, Nick, Elmira Satybaldieva, David Lewis, and John Heathershaw. "Peacebuilding and Reconciliation Projects in Southern Kyrgyzstan." Stockholm International Peace Research Institute and Open Society Foundations Working Paper, June 2014. http://www.sipri.org/research/security/afghanistan/central-asia-security/publications/sipri-osf-working-paper-megoran-et-al-june-2014 (accessed November 9, 2016).

Millar, Gearoid M. *An Ethnographic Approach to Peacebuilding: Understanding Local Experiences in Transitional States*. London: Routledge, 2014.

Millenium – Journal of International Studies. "Forum: Patrick Thaddeus Jackson the Conduct of Inquiry in International Relations." *Millenium* 41, no. 2 (2013): 247.

Minh-Ha, Trinh T. "Difference: A Special Third World Women Issue." *Feminist Review* 25, no. 1 (1987): 5–22.

Mohanty, Chandra. "Under Western Eyes: Feminist Scholarship and Colonial Discourses." *Feminist Review* 30 (1988): 61–88.

Moraga, Cherríe, and Gloria Anzaldúa, eds. *This Bridge Called My Back: Writings by Radical Women of Color*. New York: Kitchen Table, Women of Color Press, 1983.

Mosse, David. "Anti-Social Anthropology? Objectivity, Objection, and the Ethnography of Public Policy and Professional Communities." *Journal of the Royal Anthropological Institute* 12, no. 4 (2006): 935–56.

Pinker, Stephen. *The Better Angels of Our Nature*. New York: Viking, 2011.

Rancatore, Jason P. "It Is Strange: A Reply to Vrasti." *Millennium* 39, no. 1 (2010): 65–77.

Reeves, Madeleine. "Locating Danger: Konfliktologiia and the Search for Fixity in the Ferghana Valley Borderlands." *Central Asian Survey* 24, no. 1 (2005): 67–81.

Restrepo, Eduardo, and Arturo Escobar. "'Other Anthropologies and Anthropology Otherwise'. Steps to a World Anthropologies Framework." *Critique of Anthropology* 25, no. 2 (2005): 99–129.

Richmond, Oliver P. *A Post-Liberal Peace*. London: Routledge, 2011.

Richmond, Oliver P. "New Approaches to Peacebuilding." *International Peacekeeping* 21, no. 5 (2014): 696–700.

Richmond, Oliver P., and Roger Mac Ginty. "Where Now for the Critique of the Liberal Peace?" *Cooperation and Conflict* 50, no. 2 (2015): 171–89.

Richmond, Oliver P., and Audra Mitchell. *Hybrid Forms of Peace: From Everyday Agency to Post-Liberalism*. Basingstoke: Palgrave, 2011.

Richmond, Oliver P., Sandra Pogodda, and Jasmin Ramovic. "Introduction." In *The Palgrave Handbook of Disciplinary and Regional Approaches to Peace*, ed. Oliver P. Richmond, Sandra Pogodda, and Jasmin Ramovic, 1–17. Basingstoke: Palgrave, 2016.

Paffenholz, Thania. "Unpacking the Local Turn in Peacebuilding: A Critical Assessment towards an Agenda for Future Research." *Third World Quarterly* 36, no. 5 (2015): 857–74.

Sabaratnam, Meera. "IR in Dialogue … but Can We Change the Subjects? A Typology of Decolonising Strategies for the Study of World Politics." *Millennium* 39, no. 3 (2011): 781–803.

Sabaratnam, Meera. "Avatars of Eurocentrism in the Critique of the Liberal Peace." *Security Dialogue* 44, no. 3 (2013): 259–78.

Said, Edward. "Representing the Colonized: Anthropology's Interlocutors." *Critical Inquiry* 15 (Winter 1989): 205–25.

Shamudinova, Meerim K., ed. *Formirovanie tolerantnosti (pedagogika mira) - Metodicheskoe posobie dlya uchiteley* [The Formation of Tolerance (A Pedagogy of Peace) – A Methodological Guide for Teachers]. Bishkek: Institute for Public Policy, 2013.

Souillac, Geneviève, and Douglas P. Fry. "Anthropology: Implications for Peace." In *The Palgrave Handbook of Disciplinary and Regional Approaches to Peace*, ed. Oliver P. Richmond, Sandra Pogodda, and Jasmin Ramovic, 69–81. Basingstoke: Palgrave, 2016.

Spurlin, William J. "Resisting heteronormativity/resisting recolonisation: affective bonds between indigenous women in southern Africa and the difference(s) of postcolonial feminist history." *Feminist Review* 95, no. 1 (2010): 10–26.

Tishkov, Valeriy. "'Don't Kill Me, I'm a Kyrgyz!': An Anthropological Analysis of Violence in the Osh Ethnic Conflict." *Journal of Peace Research* 32, no. 2 (1995): 133–49.

Toktosunova, Adash I. "Ot redaktora [From the Editor]." *Centralnaya Asiya i Kultura Mira* [Central Asia and the Culture of Peace] 17–18 (2005): 5–6.

Turner, Mandy, and Florian P. Kühn, eds. *The Politics of International Intervention: The Tyranny of Peace*. London: Routledge, 2016.

Visoka, Gëzim. *Peace Figuration after International Intervention: Intentions, Events and Consequences of Liberal Peacebuilding*. London: Routledge, 2016.

Vrasti, Wanda. "The Strange Case of Ethnography and International Relations." *Millennium-Journal of International Studies* 37, no. 2 (2008): 279–301.

Vrasti, Wanda. "Dr Strangelove, or How I Learned to Stop Worrying about Methodology and Love Writing." *Millennium* 39, no. 1 (2010): 79–88.

Index